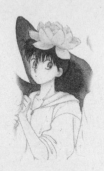

Here is Greenwood™

Vol. 2
Story and Art by
Yukie Nasu

Here is Greenwood
Vol. 2
Shôjo Edition
Story and Art by Yukie Nasu

English Adaptation/William Flanagan
Touch-up Art & Lettering/James Gaubatz
Cover and Interior Design/Izumi Evers
Editor/Michelle Pangilinan

Managing Editor/Annette Roman
Director of Production/Noboru Watanabe
Editorial Director/Alvin Lu
Sr. Director of Licensing & Acquisitions/Rika Inouye
Vice President of Sales & Marketing/Liza Coppola
Executive Vice President/Hyoe Narita
Publisher/Seiji Horibuchi

Printed in the U.S.A.

Published by VIZ, LLC
P.O. Box 77010
San Francisco, CA 94107

10 9 8 7 6 5 4 3 2 1
First printing, December 2004

store.viz.com

ANIMERICA
ANIME & MANGA MONTHLY
www.viz.com

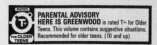
PARENTAL ADVISORY
HERE IS GREENWOOD is rated T+ for Older
Teens. This volume contains suggestive situations.
Recommended for older teens. (16 and up)

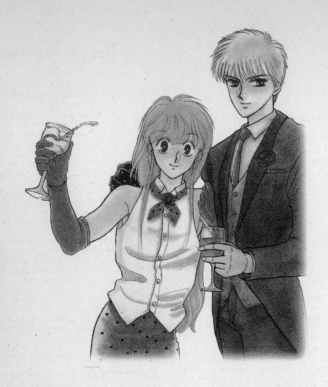

Author's Profile
Yukie Nasu

Born: Tokyo, Japan
Star Sign: Aries
Blood Type: A
Debuted in Hana to Yume, Winter
Publication with the story "U.F.
Chance." In 1986, her first
continuing series, the boy's-life story
"Here is Greenwood," became an
enormously popular signature series.
She has also published quite a few
fantasy and science fiction stories,
including "Flower Destroyer," "Yôma
Shûrai Fukushû-ki," "Gekkô," "Illusion
Food Master," and many others.

Here is Greenwood

Contents

HEADACHE
NEMESIS

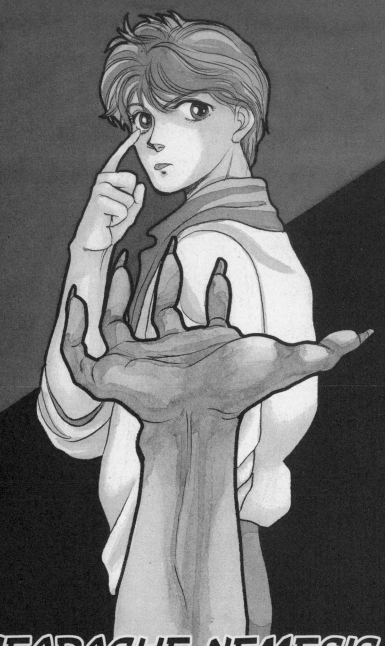

HEADACHE NEMESIS

SHUN
...
MITSURU!
RUN
!!
O-
OKAY
!!
SHREEK
KACHIK
WHA...
?
THU
!
KACHAK

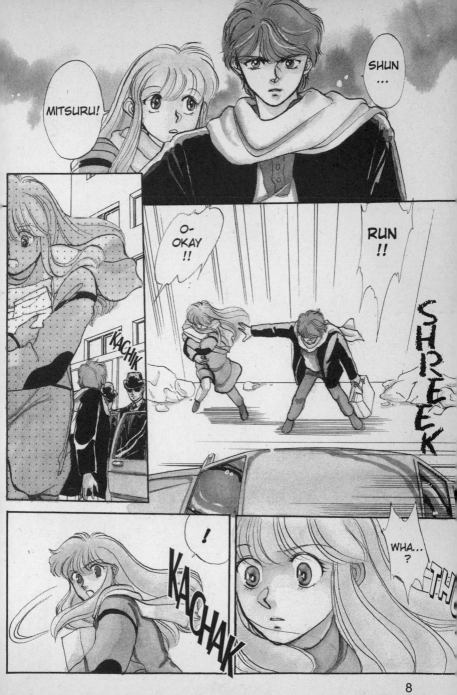

SQUEEEL
MITSURU!!
MITSURU-SEMPAI!!
MITSURU...
IT LOOKED LIKE HE WAS OUT COLD.
YOU KNOW, IT KINDA SEEMS...
...ALMOST LIKE A KIDNAPPING.
NOT "KINDA" OR "ALMOST"!
IT WAS A KIDNAPPING!!

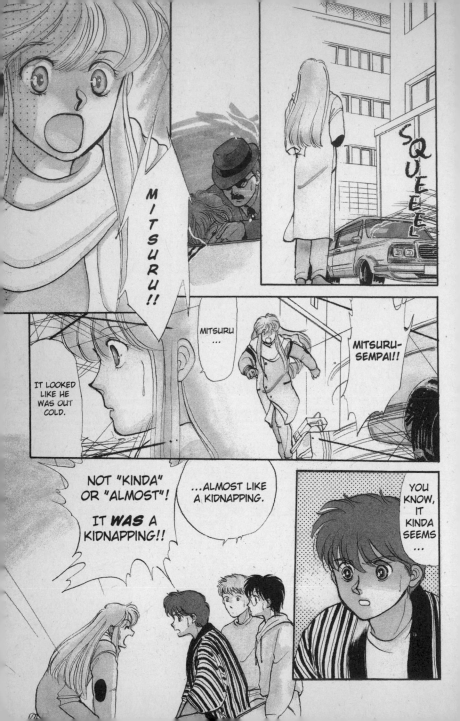

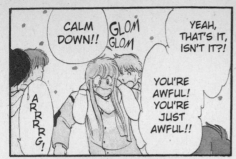

SUKA-CHAN! AREN'T YOU THE LEAST BIT WORRIED?!
EH?!
YOU WOULD JUST LOVE IT IF MITSURU WERE GONE FOREVER!!
BULL'S EYE!
YEAH, THAT'S IT, ISN'T IT?!
YOU'RE AWFUL! YOU'RE JUST AWFUL!!
GLOM GLOM
CALM DOWN!!
ARRRG!
EHHH?
.....
.....
YOU'RE ACTUALLY SERIOUS?
I HATE YOU ALL!!
WHY DO YOU GUYS --
WHAT REASON WOULD ANYBODY HAVE TO KIDNAP MITSURU?
WHO WOULD ...
I DON'T KNOW!!
EVEN I THOUGHT ... I THOUGHT FOR SURE...
... THAT IT WAS ME THEY WERE AFTER!
WHAT MAKES YOU SUCH A PRIME TARGET?
SHUN'S FAMILY RUNS A CORPORATION.
OH ... YEAH ...
AND THEN?

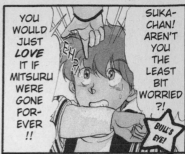

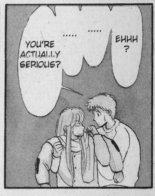

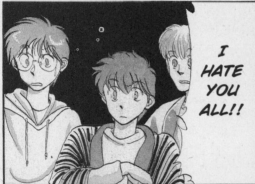

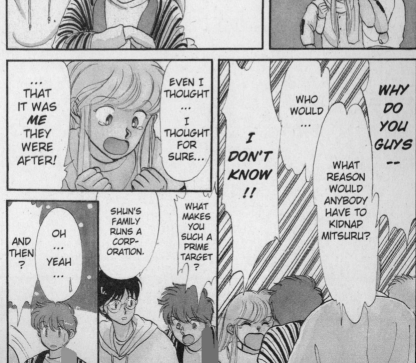

BLANK
DIDN'T THEY SAY ANYTHING?
DO YOU RE-MEM-BER ANY-THING?
WHAT KIND OF KIDNAPPERS WERE THEY?
I DON'T RE-MEMBER THINGS LIKE THAT!!
It's my fault! It's all my fault!!
SNIFF SNIFF
CRY CRY
WHINE WHINE
H-HOLD ON A SECOND.
KIDNAPPED... KIDNAPPED...
WHY WOULD ANYONE KIDNAP MITSURU?!
IF THEY WANTED A RANSOM, THEN HE'S GOOD AS DEAD.
SH-SHINOBU-SEMPAI?
EVEN IF THEY DIDN'T KNOW SHUN'S VALUE, I CAN'T IMAGINE THEM KIDNAPPING SUCH AN UNSUITABLE INDIVIDUAL FOR RANSOM.
I THINK WE'LL HAVE TO RULE OUT MONEY AS A MOTIVE.
HE NEARLY DROVE ME TO A HEART ATTACK!
IT MAY BE THEY NEED HIM FOR SOMETHING ELSE.

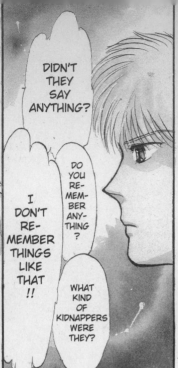

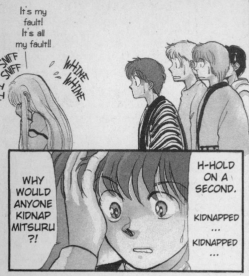

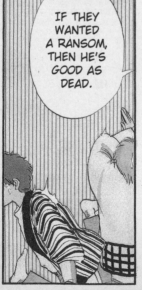

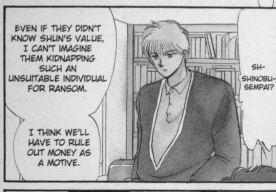

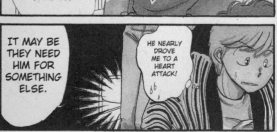

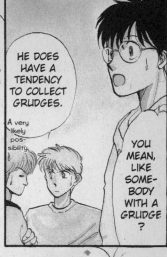

YOU MEAN, LIKE SOMEBODY WITH A GRUDGE?
HE DOES HAVE A TENDENCY TO COLLECT GRUDGES.
A very likely possibility
PERHAPS HE INJURED THE SON OF A YAKUZA DON.
AAA!!
IT COULD BE THAT HE WAS MISTAKEN FOR SOMEONE ELSE.
THAT'S HIGHLY POSSIBLE...
IT'S ALSO POSSIBLE THAT HE WAS KIDNAPPED FOR LASCIVIOUS REASONS...
LOOK, I'M BEGGING YOU! YOU DON'T HAVE TO COVER EVERY WORST-CASE SCENARIO!
IN ANY CASE, I SHOULD GET ON THE PHONE.
WITH THE POLICE?
WITH HIS FAMILY.
IF THE KIDNAPPERS WANT TO MAKE THEIR DEMANDS KNOWN...
...THE FIRST PEOPLE THEY'D CONTACT WOULD BE THEM, WOULDN'T IT?
Ryokuto Academy PTA Parent & Guardian Contact List

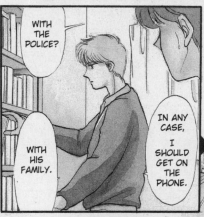

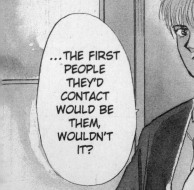

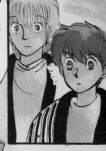

CONTACTING THE POLICE MAY PUT MITSURU'S LIFE IN DANGER.
THAT'S HIS FAMILY'S DECISION TO MAKE.
NOT OURS.
GOT IT, EVERYONE?
DON'T SAY A WORD TO ANYONE ABOUT THIS!
O-OKAY.
M-MITSURU'S LIFE?
WHY?
I'M GOING WITH YOU!
I WOULD LIKE IT IF MITSURU WEREN'T AROUND, BUT...
WHY?
WHY DOES IT HAVE TO HAPPEN LIKE THIS?!
THERE ARE WINDOWS ON THREE SIDES.
BUT THE ONLY THING I CAN SEE THROUGH THEM IS THE SKY.
IT'S ABOUT 4:00 PM, HUH?
JUST WHAT ARE THESE PEOPLE AFTER?

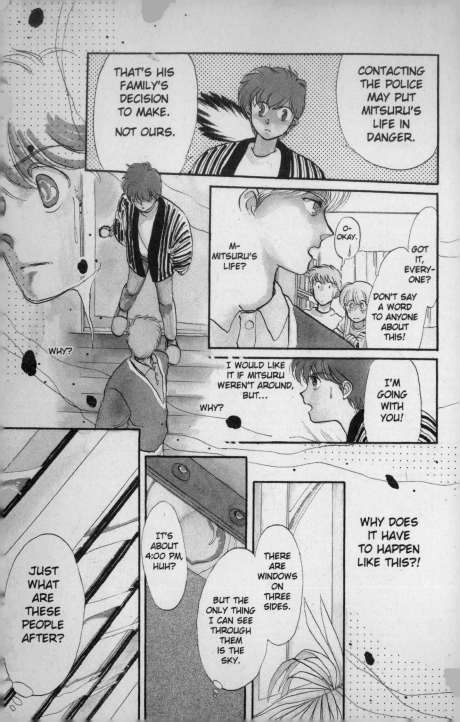

I'M IN TOKYO. THE SKY IS ALWAYS THAT COLOR HERE.
WHICH MEANS THAT I'M ON THE TOP FLOOR OF A TALL APARTMENT BUILDING OR A HOTEL.
AT LEAST THESE GUYS AREN'T HURTING FOR MONEY.
THESE FURNISHINGS LOOK LIKE THEY COST A FORTUNE!
IF THEY WERE AFTER MONEY, SHUN OR SHINOBU WOULD HAVE BEEN BETTER TARGETS.
WHAT CAN THEY BE AFTER?
I WAS CERTAIN THEY WERE TRYING TO KIDNAP SHUN!
STRGG! STRGG!
MAYBE YOU'RE AWAKE NOW?
!

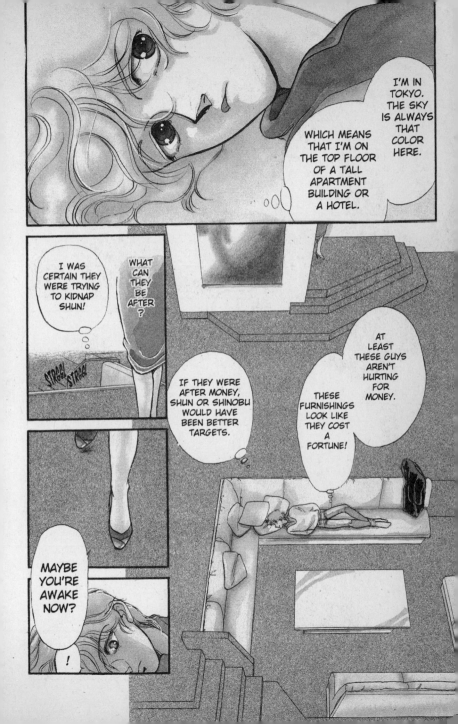

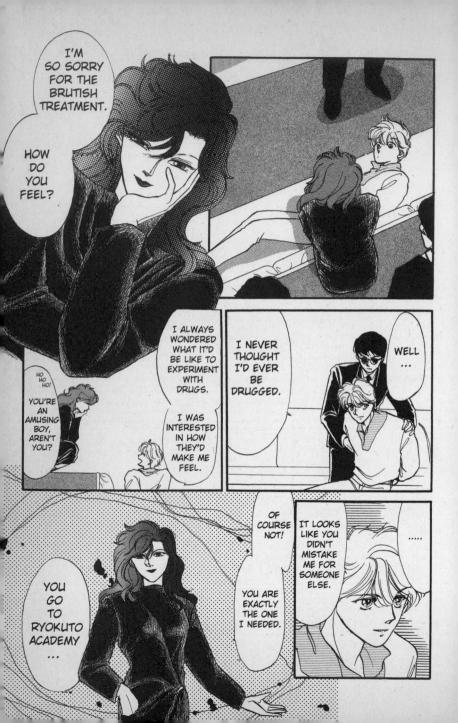

I'M SO SORRY FOR THE BRUTISH TREATMENT.
HOW DO YOU FEEL?
WELL ...
I NEVER THOUGHT I'D EVER BE DRUGGED.
I ALWAYS WONDERED WHAT IT'D BE LIKE TO EXPERIMENT WITH DRUGS.
I WAS INTERESTED IN HOW THEY'D MAKE ME FEEL.
HO HO HO!
YOU'RE AN AMUSING BOY, AREN'T YOU?
.....
IT LOOKS LIKE YOU DIDN'T MISTAKE ME FOR SOMEONE ELSE.
OF COURSE NOT!
YOU ARE EXACTLY THE ONE I NEEDED.
YOU GO TO RYOKUTO ACADEMY ...

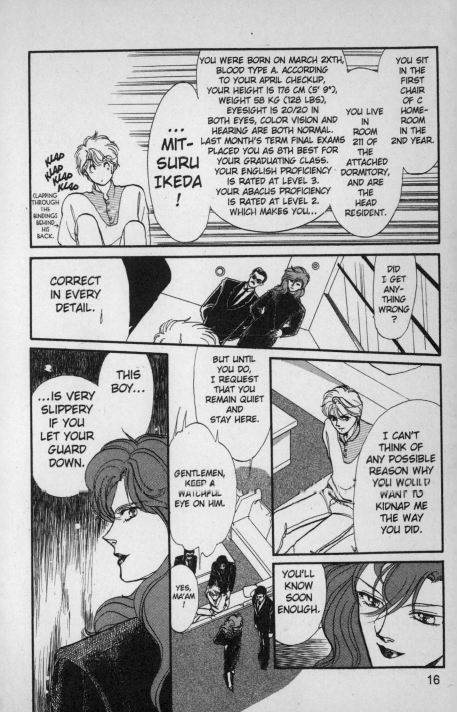

YOU SIT IN THE FIRST CHAIR OF C HOME-ROOM IN THE 2ND YEAR.
YOU LIVE IN ROOM 211 OF THE ATTACHED DORMITORY, AND ARE THE HEAD RESIDENT.
YOU WERE BORN ON MARCH 2XTH, BLOOD TYPE A. ACCORDING TO YOUR APRIL CHECKUP, YOUR HEIGHT IS 176 CM (5' 9"), WEIGHT 58 KG (128 LBS), EYESIGHT IS 20/20 IN BOTH EYES, COLOR VISION AND HEARING ARE BOTH NORMAL. LAST MONTH'S TERM FINAL EXAMS PLACED YOU AS 8TH BEST FOR YOUR GRADUATING CLASS. YOUR ENGLISH PROFICIENCY IS RATED AT LEVEL 3. YOUR ABACUS PROFICIENCY IS RATED AT LEVEL 2. WHICH MAKES YOU...
... MIT-SURU IKEDA !
KLAP KLAP KLAP KLAP
CLAPPING THROUGH THE BINDINGS BEHIND HIS BACK.
DID I GET ANY-THING WRONG ?
CORRECT IN EVERY DETAIL.
I CAN'T THINK OF ANY POSSIBLE REASON WHY YOU WOULD WANT TO KIDNAP ME THE WAY YOU DID.
YOU'LL KNOW SOON ENOUGH.
BUT UNTIL YOU DO, I REQUEST THAT YOU REMAIN QUIET AND STAY HERE.
GENTLEMEN, KEEP A WATCHFUL EYE ON HIM.
YES, MA'AM !
THIS BOY...
...IS VERY SLIPPERY IF YOU LET YOUR GUARD DOWN.

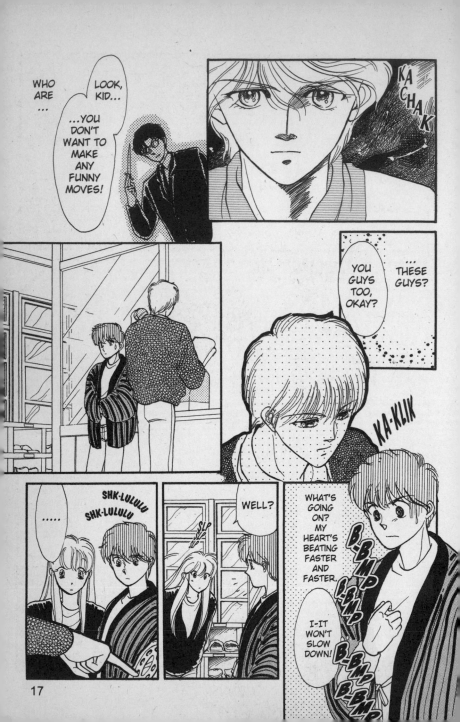

WHO ARE ...

LOOK, KID...

...YOU DON'T WANT TO MAKE ANY FUNNY MOVES!

KA CHAK

...THESE GUYS?

YOU GUYS TOO, OKAY?

KA-KLIK

......

SHK-LULULU
SHK-LULULU

WELL?

SLP

WHAT'S GOING ON? MY HEART'S BEATING FASTER AND FASTER.

I-IT WON'T SLOW DOWN!

B-BMP
B-BMP
B-BMP
B-BMP

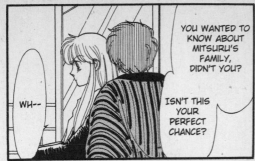

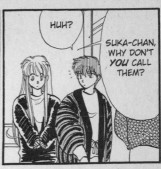

HUH?
SUKA-CHAN, WHY DON'T *YOU* CALL THEM?
YOU WANTED TO KNOW ABOUT MITSURU'S FAMILY, DIDN'T YOU?
ISN'T THIS YOUR PERFECT CHANCE?
WH--
WHAT ARE YOU TALKING ABOUT? THIS IS NOT THE TIME...
YOU DON'T CARE WHAT HAPPENS TO MITSURU, RIGHT?
IF HE'S NOT HERE, HE CAN'T TORMENT YOU.
YOU'LL FINALLY GET ALL THE FOOD YOU PAID FOR.
¡BU--
PICK PICK PICK PICK
MASSIVE VENTING
OR CAN YOU POSSIBLY BE WORRIED? REALLY WORRIED? CAN YOU *ACTUALLY* BE INTERESTED IN SEEING HIM BACK SAFELY?
CHK
HELLO?
WHEN DID I *EVER* SAY THAT--
GASP
HELLO? IKEDA RESIDENCE?
IS THAT YOU, SHÔ?
OH! SHINOBU?
YES. IT'S BEEN A WHILE.
NICE TO HEAR FROM YOU.

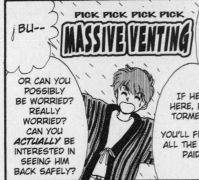

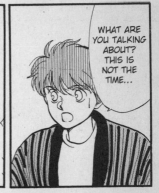

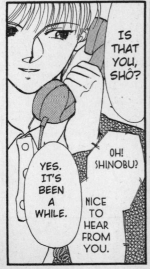

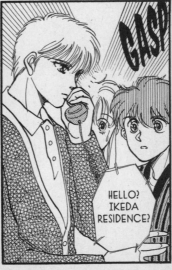

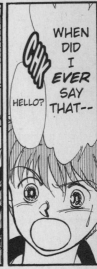

HOW'S YOUR MOM DOING?
SHINOBU!
WHY ARE YOU TALKING LIKE THIS IS SOME SOCIAL CALL?!
IS SOMETHING WRONG?
NOTHING AT ALL.
IS MITSURU OVER THERE?
NO.
DID SOMETHING HAPPEN TO HIM?
NO. I JUST HAD SOMETHING TO DISCUSS WITH HIM, BUT HE'S OUT. I THOUGHT MAYBE HE'D BE HOME.
IF HE DOES COME HOME, PLEASE ASK HIM TO CALL ME HERE.
SHINOBU?
I APPRECIATE IT.
YES.
GOOD-BYE.
KACHAK
SHINOBU, WHY WOULD YOU...

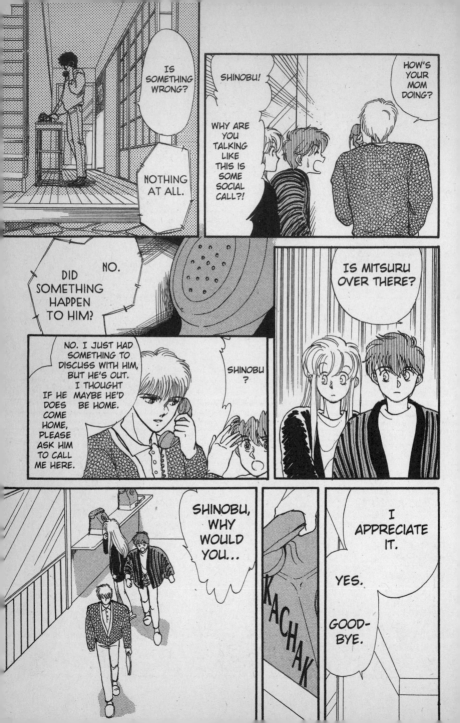

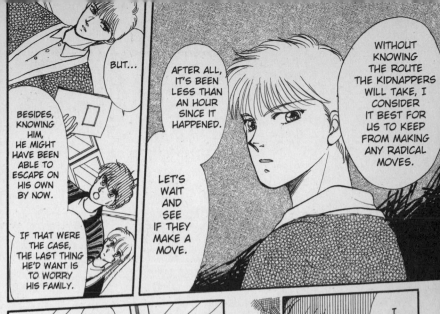

WITHOUT KNOWING THE ROUTE THE KIDNAPPERS WILL TAKE, I CONSIDER IT BEST FOR US TO KEEP FROM MAKING ANY RADICAL MOVES.
AFTER ALL, IT'S BEEN LESS THAN AN HOUR SINCE IT HAPPENED.
LET'S WAIT AND SEE IF THEY MAKE A MOVE.
BUT...
BESIDES, KNOWING HIM, HE MIGHT HAVE BEEN ABLE TO ESCAPE ON HIS OWN BY NOW.
IF THAT WERE THE CASE, THE LAST THING HE'D WANT IS TO WORRY HIS FAMILY.
I GUESS THAT'S TRUE...
MAYBE HE'S RIGHT...
IT *IS* MITSURU, SO HE'LL PROBABLY STILL BE ALL RIGHT.
THEN... WHOM DID YOU TALK TO ON THE PHONE?
I HAPPENED TO OVERHEAR IT...
YOU MEAN SHÔ?
SHÔ IS MITSURU'S YOUNGER BROTHER. HE GOES TO A DIFFERENT HIGH SCHOOL...
SHINOBU, YOU KNOW ABOUT MITSURU'S HOME LIFE?
I'VE SLEPT OVER THERE BEFORE.
WH-WHAT'S THAT LOOK FOR? I WAS ONLY ASKING!
STARE
SHUN...
...YOU MIGHT WANT TO STOP VENTING YOUR ANGER ON HASUKAWA.
RELATIVELY ADEPT AT GIVING THE EVIL EYE.

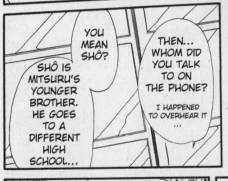

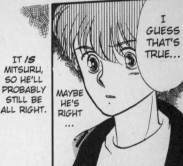

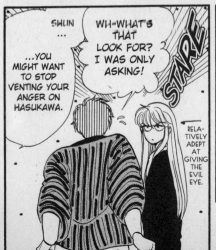

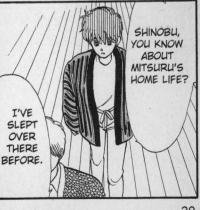

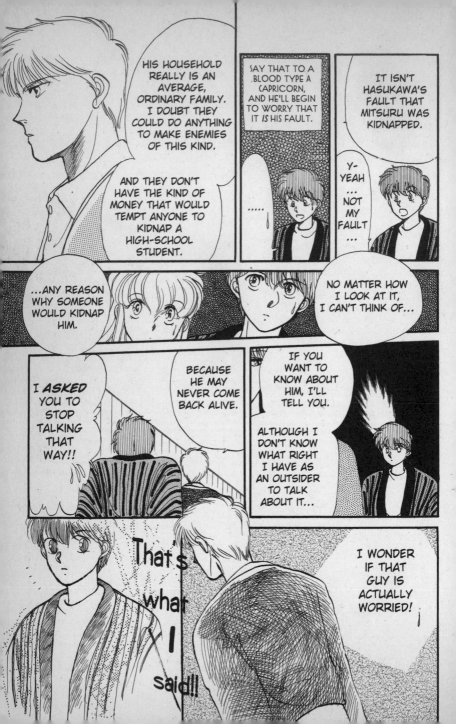

IT ISN'T HASUKAWA'S FAULT THAT MITSURU WAS KIDNAPPED.
Y-YEAH ... NOT MY FAULT ...
SAY THAT TO A BLOOD TYPE A CAPRICORN, AND HE'LL BEGIN TO WORRY THAT IT *IS* HIS FAULT.
.....
HIS HOUSEHOLD REALLY IS AN AVERAGE, ORDINARY FAMILY. I DOUBT THEY COULD DO ANYTHING TO MAKE ENEMIES OF THIS KIND.
AND THEY DON'T HAVE THE KIND OF MONEY THAT WOULD TEMPT ANYONE TO KIDNAP A HIGH-SCHOOL STUDENT.
NO MATTER HOW I LOOK AT IT, I CAN'T THINK OF...
...ANY REASON WHY SOMEONE WOULD KIDNAP HIM.
IF YOU WANT TO KNOW ABOUT HIM, I'LL TELL YOU.
ALTHOUGH I DON'T KNOW WHAT RIGHT I HAVE AS AN OUTSIDER TO TALK ABOUT IT...
BECAUSE HE MAY NEVER COME BACK ALIVE.
I ***ASKED*** YOU TO STOP TALKING THAT WAY!!
I WONDER IF THAT GUY IS ACTUALLY WORRIED!
That's what I said!!

WA HA HA
NOBODY KNOWS YET...
IF THEY KNEW ...
...THAT THEIR SEMPAI, MITSURU, ISN'T HERE.
URK!
B-BMP B-BMP B-BMP B-BMP B-BMP B-BMP
THEN ...
I WONDER WHAT THEY'D DO.

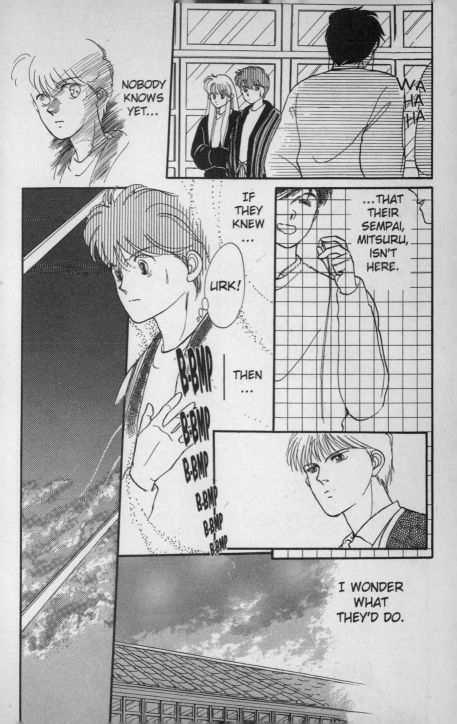

I THINK IT'S TIME ...
...TO GIVE THE BOY A LITTLE SCARE, HMM?
ALTHOUGH I REGRET NOT BEING ABLE TO SEE IT FOR MYSELF.
I HOPE HE FINDS ME!
GO HO HO HO HO!
WHAT?
FORGIVE MY INTRU- SION.
WE'VE PREPARED THE HOSTAGE'S MEAL.
DO WE HAVE PER- MISSION TO SERVE IT?
YOU KIDNAPPED ME JUST AS I WAS BRINGING LUNCH HOME TO EAT.
AND THE WHOLE AFTERNOON HAS BEEN PRETTY TAXING.
I'M HUNGRY, OKAY?
YOU DON'T GET WHO'S IN CHARGE HERE, DO YOU?

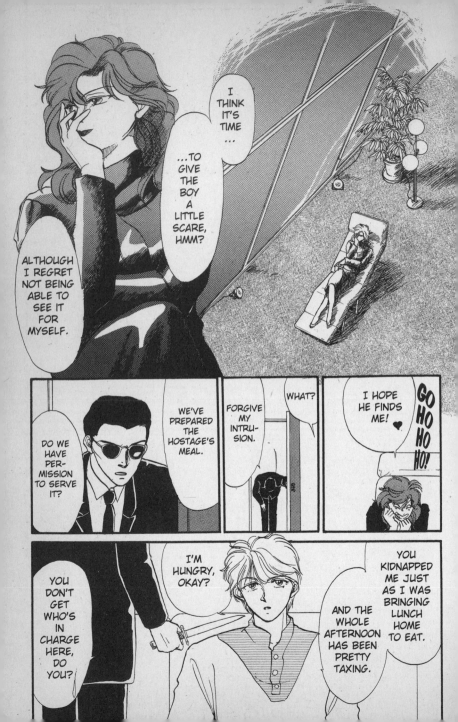

THEY'RE RIGHT. YOU DO HAVE GUTS.
AS A HOSTAGE, I'M AFRAID YOU'LL HAVE TO PUT UP WITH CERTAIN INCONVENIENCES.
AND...
...IF YOU WHINE TOO MUCH IN HUNGER, IT WOULD BE A SHAME TO RUIN THE LOOKS OF A FINE YOUNG MAN.
WELL SAID— HOWEVER ...
...WITHOUT FOOD, MY LOOKS WILL FADE QUITE QUICKLY.
THIS IS ENTERTAINING. IN WHAT WAY WILL YOUR LOOKS FADE?
THIS WAY.
FWAK
B-BMP B-BMP B-BMP B-BM B-BM B-BMP
SOME-BODY ... GIVE THE BOY SOME FOOD!!
HUH?
UM...
I DIDN'T WANT TO HAVE TO PUT ON THAT FACE, BUT...
HUH?
IS THAT A COMPLAINT I HEAR?
YOU'D THINK A WOMAN WOULD BE ABLE TO COOK FOR HERSELF!

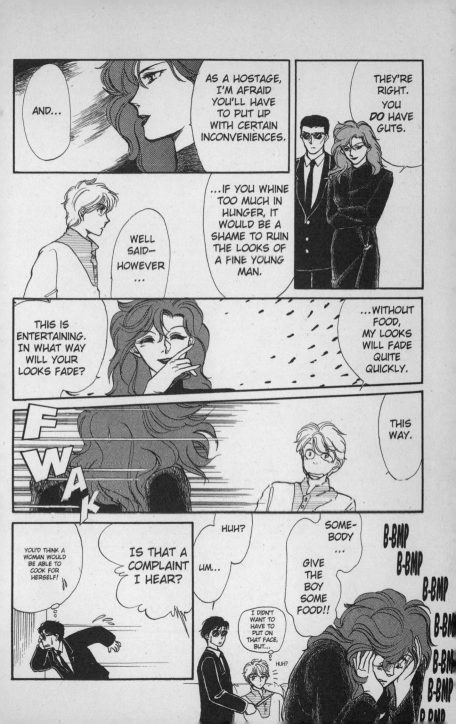

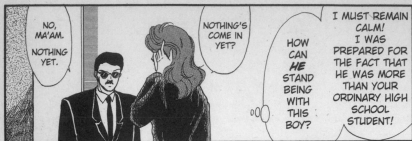

I MUST REMAIN CALM! I WAS PREPARED FOR THE FACT THAT HE WAS MORE THAN YOUR ORDINARY HIGH SCHOOL STUDENT!
HOW CAN **HE** STAND BEING WITH THIS BOY?
NOTHING'S COME IN YET?
NO, MA'AM.
NOTHING YET.
PERHAPS IT'S TIME TO LET YOU IN ON IT.
YOU MEAN THE REASON WHY YOU KIDNAPPED ME AND BROUGHT ME HERE?
I'D APPRECIATE IT IF THIS WAS OVER BY THE DORM'S CURFEW.
THAT'S TRUE.
IT WOULDN'T DO FOR THE HEAD RESIDENT TO BE AWOL FROM HIS OWN DORM.
BUT...
I'M AFRAID WE CANNOT RETURN YOU YET.
NOT UNTIL **HE** COMES HERE.
"HE"?
WHO?
HE'S ...
... SOMEONE YOU KNOW WELL.

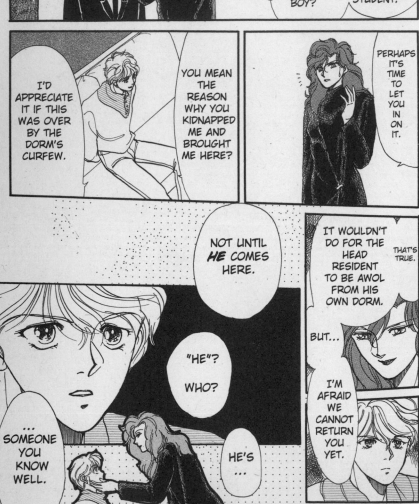

YOU SEE, I...
...TOOK A HOSTAGE TO GET REVENGE ON THAT MAN.
CAN YOU GUESS WHO?
NOT A CLUE TO WHO HE IS, BUT I FEEL SORRY FOR HIM!
CHATTR
CHATTR
WHAT'S WRONG? WHY DON'T THE KIDNAPPERS SAY SOMETHING?
NO...
KLAK
THEY DON'T CALL ...
THIS IS NO GOOD. MY THROAT'S TOO TIGHT TO EAT.
CHOMP
SHINOBU ...

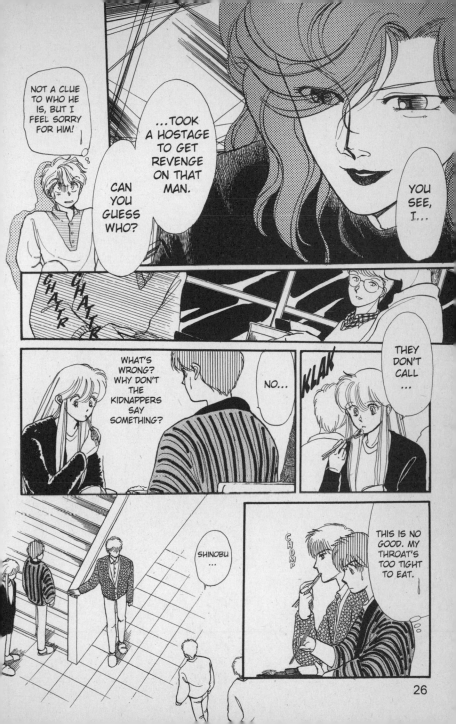

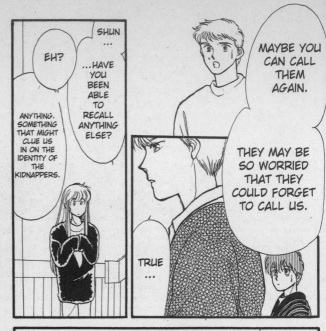

MAYBE YOU CAN CALL THEM AGAIN.
THEY MAY BE SO WORRIED THAT THEY COULD FORGET TO CALL US.
TRUE ...
SHUN ...
...HAVE YOU BEEN ABLE TO RECALL ANYTHING ELSE?
EH?
ANYTHING. SOMETHING THAT MIGHT CLUE US IN ON THE IDENTITY OF THE KIDNAPPERS.
UM...
UH...
ER...
THE CAR WAS BIG, AND IT WAS A FOREIGN MAKE...

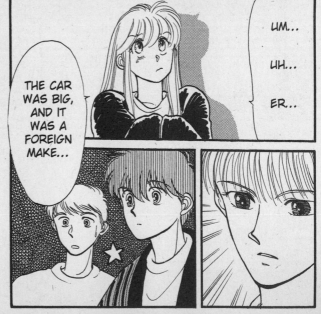

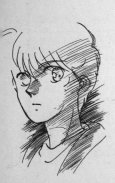

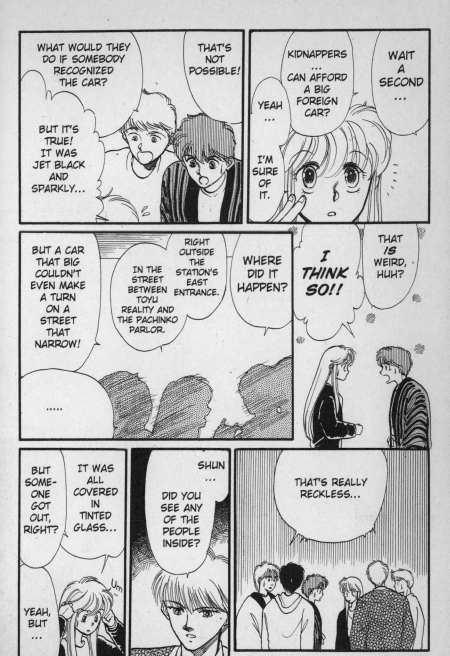

WAIT A SECOND...
KIDNAPPERS... CAN AFFORD A BIG FOREIGN CAR?
YEAH... I'M SURE OF IT.
THAT'S NOT POSSIBLE!
WHAT WOULD THEY DO IF SOMEBODY RECOGNIZED THE CAR?
BUT IT'S TRUE! IT WAS JET BLACK AND SPARKLY...
THAT IS WEIRD, HUH?
I THINK SO!!
WHERE DID IT HAPPEN?
RIGHT OUTSIDE THE STATION'S EAST ENTRANCE.
IN THE STREET BETWEEN TOYU REALITY AND THE PACHINKO PARLOR.
BUT A CAR THAT BIG COULDN'T EVEN MAKE A TURN ON A STREET THAT NARROW!
.....
THAT'S REALLY RECKLESS...
SHUN... DID YOU SEE ANY OF THE PEOPLE INSIDE?
IT WAS ALL COVERED IN TINTED GLASS...
BUT SOME-ONE GOT OUT, RIGHT?
Um...
YEAH, BUT...

I COULDN'T SEE ANYTHING WITH THEIR BLACK HATS, BLACK SUNGLASSES, BLACK SUITS AND BLACK SHOES...
THAT'S JUST DUMB!!
CRIMINALS IN SUSPICIOUS CLOTHING LIKE THAT? IT DOESN'T HAPPEN IN REAL LIFE!
.....
BUT THAT'S EXACTLY HOW IT HAPPENED!!
ISN'T THE WAY THEY DID IT A LITTLE OVERBOARD?
YOU DON'T THINK THEY REALLY ...
... ARE DEVIANTS?
It's almost as if I can see through the manga artist's eyes, and it scares me!
GUYS DRESSED IN BLACK DRIVE UP IN A BIG, CONSPICUOUS, FOREIGN CAR AND KIDNAP SOMEONE IN BROAD DAYLIGHT. IT'S A SCRIPT FILLED WITH DUMB CLICHES.
Idiot!
Ow! That hurts!
Fool!
IT'S A PLAN WITH A PATHETIC LACK OF ORIGINALITY AND, IN ADDITION, THEY KIDNAPPED MITSURU IKEDA, A MAN WITH NO REASON TO BE KIDNAPPED.
VERY FEW PEOPLE IN THE WORLD MIGHT DO SUCH A THING...
...AND I THINK I KNOW ONE OF 'EM.

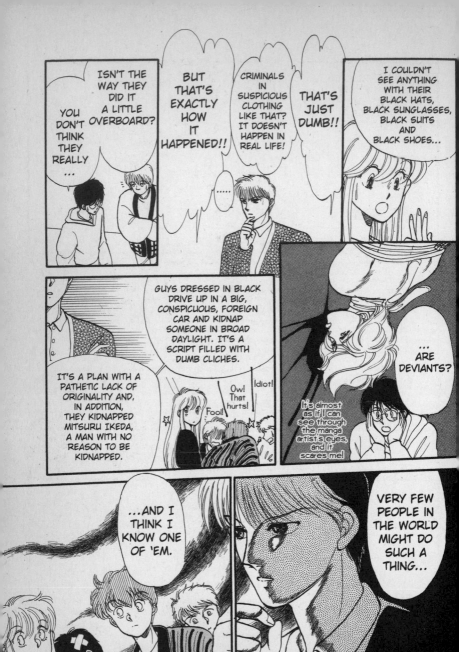

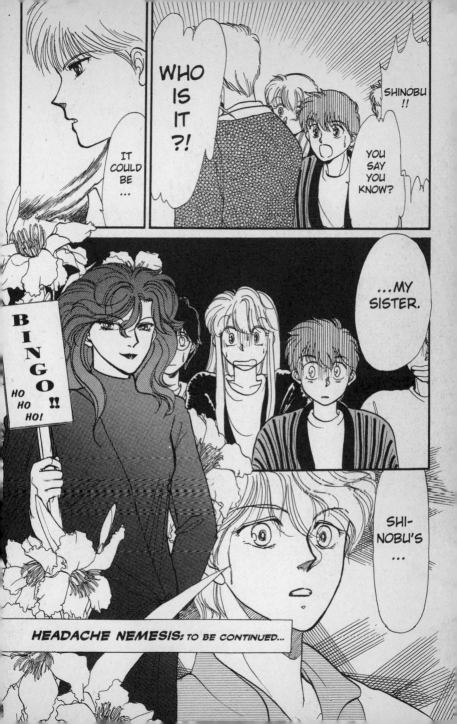

WHO IS IT?!

IT COULD BE...

SHINOBU!!

YOU SAY YOU KNOW?

...MY SISTER.

BINGO HO HO HO!!

SHI- NOBU'S...

HEADACHE NEMESIS: TO BE CONTINUED...

HEADACHE NEMESIS
What kind of title page is this supposed to be?

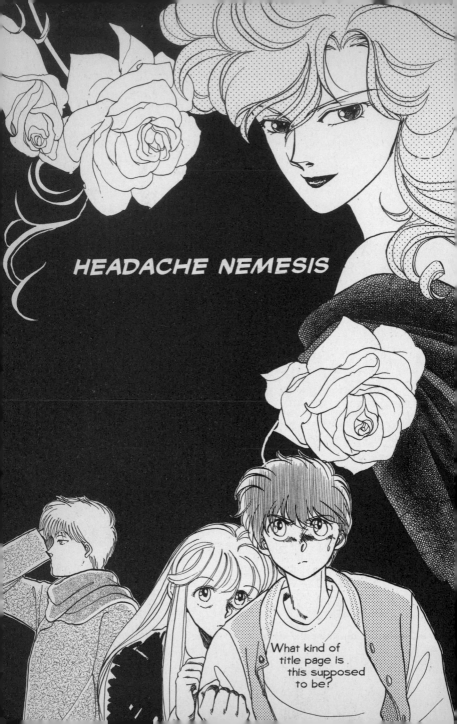

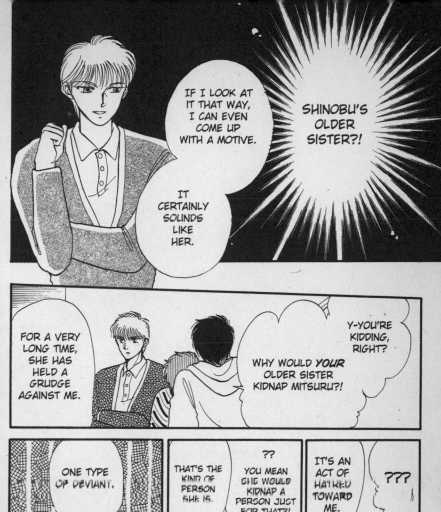

SHINOBU'S OLDER SISTER?!
IF I LOOK AT IT THAT WAY, I CAN EVEN COME UP WITH A MOTIVE.
IT CERTAINLY SOUNDS LIKE HER.
Y-YOU'RE KIDDING, RIGHT?
WHY WOULD *YOUR* OLDER SISTER KIDNAP MITSURU?!
FOR A VERY LONG TIME, SHE HAS HELD A GRUDGE AGAINST ME.
???
IT'S AN ACT OF HATRED TOWARD ME.
??
YOU MEAN SHE WOULD KIDNAP A PERSON JUST FOR THAT?!
THAT'S THE KIND OF PERSON SHE IS.
WHAT KIND OF PERSON IS THAT?!
ONE TYPE OF DEVIANT.

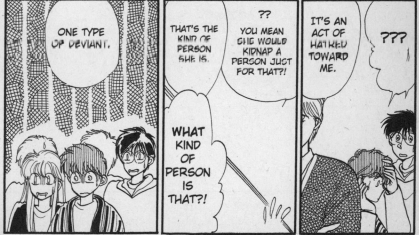

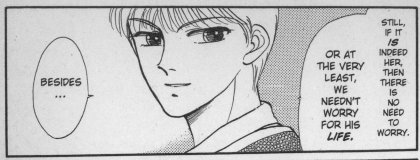

STILL, IF IT *IS* INDEED HER, THEN THERE IS NO NEED TO WORRY.
OR AT THE VERY LEAST, WE NEEDN'T WORRY FOR HIS *LIFE.*
BESIDES ...
HE'S A MAN WHO SOLD HIS VIRGINITY FOR 10,000 YEN WHEN HE WAS 11 YEARS OLD, RIGHT?
WAAAAAAAAA?!
SHINOBU, DO YOU KNOW WHERE SHE IS? WE HAVE TO GO THERE!
I DOUBT SHE WOULD STILL BE LIVING IN HER PREVIOUS APART-MENT.
BUT NOT TO WORRY.
WE'LL KNOW EVERYTHING SOON ENOUGH.
HA HA HA
SEMPAI !!
WHAT KIND OF WOMAN DO YOU THINK SHINOBU'S SISTER IS?
I'D BE WILLING TO BELIEVE ANYTHING RIGHT NOW!
NOW THAT YOU MENTION IT, HE DID TELL ME ABOUT HIS FAMILY.

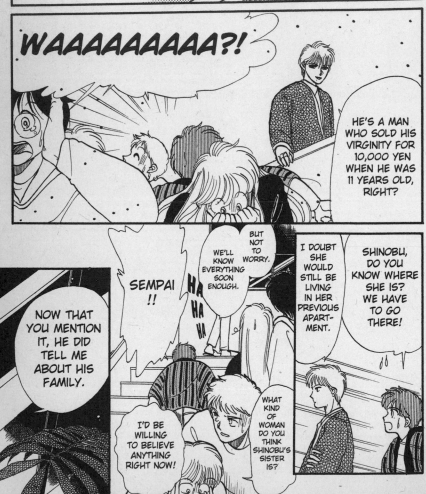

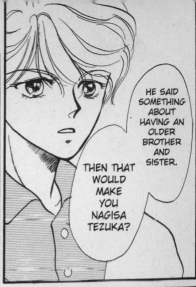

HE SAID SOMETHING ABOUT HAVING AN OLDER BROTHER AND SISTER.
THEN THAT WOULD MAKE YOU NAGISA TEZUKA?
YES. I SEE YOU'RE ... ... WELL IN-FORMED.
FOR A WOMAN TO WANT REVENGE ON HER LITTLE BROTHER ...
...I DOUBT YOU COULD EVER UNDERSTAND HOW CIRCUMSTANCES COULD LEAD TO THAT.
SURE I CAN.
I UNDERSTAND IT PERFECTLY. LIVING WITH A MAN LIKE THAT FOR 16 YEARS, IT WOULD BE UNUSUAL NOT TO HATE HIM AT LEAST A LITTLE...
SHUT UP !!
HOW COULD YOU...
HOW COULD ANYONE UNDERSTAND?! THE PAIN AND SUFFERING I HAD TO ENDURE DAY AFTER DAY—NOBODY ELSE CAN KNOW WHAT THAT'S LIKE!!
I THOUGHT YOU WANTED ME TO SYMPATHIZE.

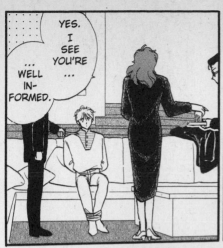

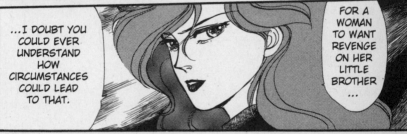

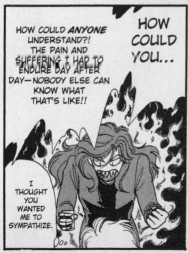

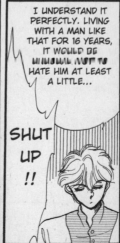

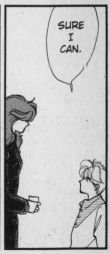

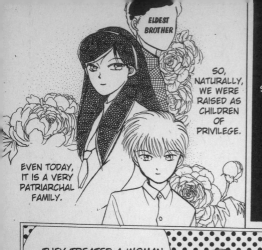

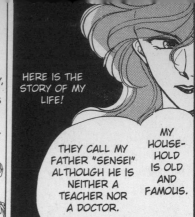

HERE IS THE STORY OF MY LIFE!
MY HOUSE-HOLD IS OLD AND FAMOUS.
THEY CALL MY FATHER "SENSEI" ALTHOUGH HE IS NEITHER A TEACHER NOR A DOCTOR.
ELDEST BROTHER
SO, NATURALLY, WE WERE RAISED AS CHILDREN OF PRIVILEGE.
EVEN TODAY, IT IS A VERY PATRIARCHAL FAMILY.
COMPARED TO MY ELDEST BROTHER, AKIRA...
3
2
...THEY TREATED A WOMAN SUCH AS ME, OR A SECOND SON SUCH AS SHINOBU, WITH CRIMINAL NEGLECT.
I CANNOT FORGIVE MY FATHER...
...FOR TREATING SHINOBU AND MYSELF AS INFERIOR HUMAN BEINGS!!
I WORKED AS HARD AS I COULD...
AS LONG AS AKIRA WAS THERE, IT WAS MY FATE TO BE MARRIED OFF TO SOMEONE. I KNEW THAT, BUT STILL I WORKED.
BUT SHINOBU WAS QUITE DIFFERENT.
WHILE AKIRA AND I WORKED UNTIL WE SWEATED BLOOD, *HE* WENT THROUGH LIFE UNCONCERNED. AS IF HIS WINNING WAS SOMETHING ALREADY DECIDED.
HE ACTED AS IF *HE* WERE THE NATURAL HEIR, AND HE JUST FLOATED THROUGH LIFE.

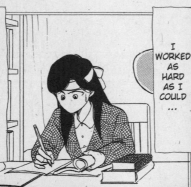

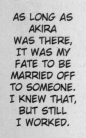

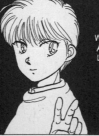

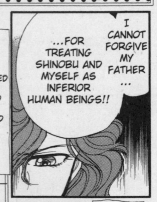

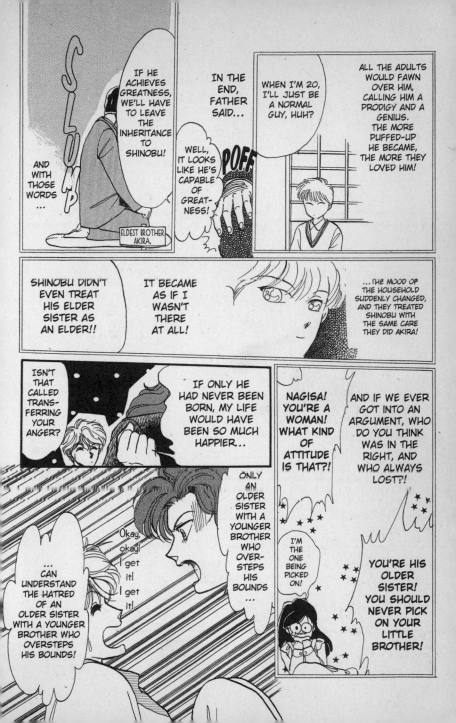

ALL THE ADULTS WOULD FAWN OVER HIM, CALLING HIM A PRODIGY AND A GENIUS. THE MORE PUFFED-UP HE BECAME, THE MORE THEY LOVED HIM!
WHEN I'M 20, I'LL JUST BE A NORMAL GUY, HUH?
IN THE END, FATHER SAID...
WELL, IT LOOKS LIKE HE'S CAPABLE OF GREAT-NESS!
POFF
IF HE ACHIEVES GREATNESS, WE'LL HAVE TO LEAVE THE INHERITANCE TO SHINOBU!
SLUMP
ELDEST BROTHER AKIRA.
AND WITH THOSE WORDS ...
...THE MOOD OF THE HOUSEHOLD SUDDENLY CHANGED, AND THEY TREATED SHINOBU WITH THE SAME CARE THEY DID AKIRA!
IT BECAME AS IF I WASN'T THERE AT ALL!
SHINOBU DIDN'T EVEN TREAT HIS ELDER SISTER AS AN ELDER!!
AND IF WE EVER GOT INTO AN ARGUMENT, WHO DO YOU THINK WAS IN THE RIGHT, AND WHO ALWAYS LOST?!
NAGISA! YOU'RE A WOMAN! WHAT KIND OF ATTITUDE IS THAT?!
YOU'RE HIS OLDER SISTER! YOU SHOULD NEVER PICK ON YOUR LITTLE BROTHER!
I'M THE ONE BEING PICKED ON!
IF ONLY HE HAD NEVER BEEN BORN, MY LIFE WOULD HAVE BEEN SO MUCH HAPPIER...
ISN'T THAT CALLED TRANS-FERRING YOUR ANGER?
ONLY AN OLDER SISTER WITH A YOUNGER BROTHER WHO OVER-STEPS HIS BOUNDS ...
... CAN UNDERSTAND THE HATRED OF AN OLDER SISTER WITH A YOUNGER BROTHER WHO OVERSTEPS HIS BOUNDS!
Okay, okay! I get it! I get it!

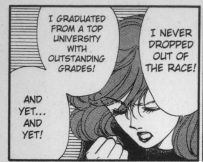

AND WITH THAT, MY BIG BROTHER AKIRA, FRIGHTENED THAT HE COULDN'T TAKE LIVING UNDER THE PRESSURE OF EVERYONE'S EXPECTATIONS, WENT INTO FULL RETREAT.
THE ENTIRE FAMILY, FROM THE HOUSE-HOLD TO DIS-TANT RELATIVES, SIMPLY ASSUMED THAT SHINOBU WAS THE ONE TO INHERIT EVERYTHING.
AND THEY TOTALLY DISRE-GARDED HIS OLDER SISTER.
I GRADUATED FROM A TOP UNIVERSITY WITH OUTSTANDING GRADES!
I NEVER DROPPED OUT OF THE RACE!
AND YET... AND YET!
WHY MUST I BE SO OPPRESSED, JUST BECAUSE I'M A WOMAN?!
OH, MISS NAGISA!
SNIFF SNIFF
I DOUBT IT'S *JUST* BECAUSE YOU'RE A WOMAN.
WELL... WE'LL SET ASIDE THE DISCUSSION OF MY FAMILY FOR THE MOMENT.
I'VE ALREADY RESIGNED MYSELF TO IT.
GULP
IT'S JUST ...
...I'VE FINALLY COME TO THE CONCLUSION THAT I WILL FIND NO PEACE UNTIL I MAKE THAT BOY SUFFER!
I'VE KNOWN THIS FOR A WHILE NOW.
I UNDERSTOOD THAT ATTACKING HIM DIRECTLY IS NOT IN MY BEST INTEREST.
SO WHAT TO DO?
THAT'S RIGHT!
ATTACK THE THINGS HE CARES ABOUT!
THAT FITS WITH THE THEORIES OF SIBLING AGGRESSION.
IT DOES?

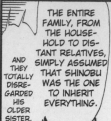

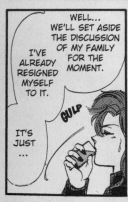

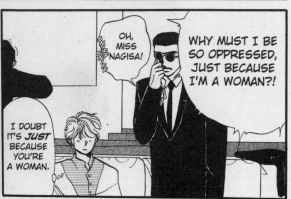

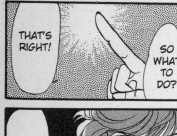

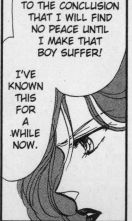

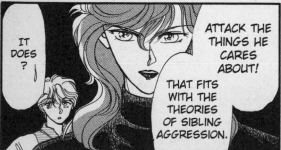

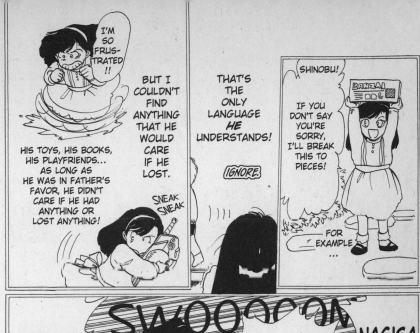

FOR EXAMPLE ...
SHINOBU!
IF YOU DON'T SAY YOU'RE SORRY, I'LL BREAK THIS TO PIECES!
BANZAI
THAT'S THE ONLY LANGUAGE HE UNDERSTANDS!
IGNORE.
BUT I COULDN'T FIND ANYTHING THAT HE WOULD CARE IF HE LOST.
SNEAK SNEAK
I'M SO FRUS-TRATED !!
HIS TOYS, HIS BOOKS, HIS PLAYFRIENDS... AS LONG AS HE WAS IN FATHER'S FAVOR, HE DIDN'T CARE IF HE HAD ANYTHING OR LOST ANYTHING!
NAGISA !!
I'VE TOLD YOU TIME AND TIME AGAIN NOT TO TAKE THINGS THAT AREN'T YOURS!!
SWOOOOOON
AND STILL YOU DON'T UNDERSTAND!
HE DIDN'T HAVE A SINGLE WEAKNESS!
I COULD DO NOTHING BUT STAND BY AND TAKE IT!
AND ALL THE WHILE, NOTHING I DID COULD EVEN BUDGE THAT SELF-SATISFIED SMIRK THAT HE USES TO DECEIVE EVERYONE AROUND HIM!
AND NOW HE'S THE STUDENT BODY PRESIDENT?!
WHY DON'T PEOPLE UNDER-STAND THAT HE'S PUTTING ONE OVER ALL OF YOU?!
A PERSON'S WEAKNESS IS SOMETHING THAT THE PERSON WOULD NOT WANT TO LOSE!
SO A MAN WITH NO WEAKNESS IS A MAN WHO LOVES NOTHING!

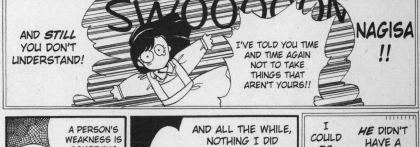

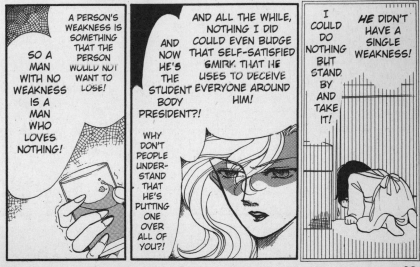

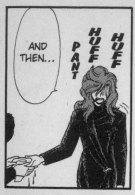

HOW CAN THEY STAND TO HAVE A DEMON LIKE HIM LEAD THEM?!
I'D NEVER STAND FOR IT! NEVER, NEVER STAND FOR IT!!
CHASHH
MISS NAGISA!
HUFF HUFF
PANT
AND THEN...
...DURING NEW YEAR'S, HE RETURNED HOME AFTER QUITE SOME TIME.
SHINOBU, HAVE YOU FOUND ANYTHING INCONVENIENT ABOUT LIVING IN TOKYO?
NOTHING IN PARTICULAR.
BUT THERE WAS NO REASON FOR YOU TO LIVE IN A DORM!!
BEING FORCED TO SLEEP IN THE SAME ROOM AS SOME NOBODY COMMONER FROM GOD-KNOWS-WHERE!
THE ELDERLY WOMAN IS PROBABLY THE CHILD OF AN OLD ARISTOCRATIC FAMILY.
THE "NOBODY" YOU'RE REFERRING TO...
...IS A MAN NAMED MITSURU IKEDA.
AND A FRIEND OF MINE.
A NOBODY WITH QUITE A HEALTHY BODY.

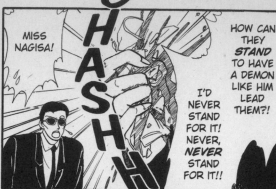

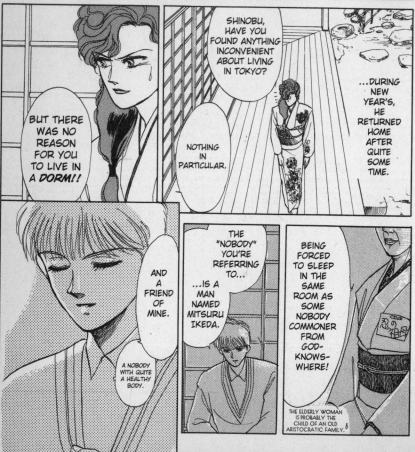

IS THAT SO?
WELL, I HOPE I CAN MEET HIM SOMEDAY.
Okay, with a family like that influencing you, I can see how his personality came about.
WHAT A LAUGH!
I NEVER THOUGHT THAT I WOULD HEAR THE WORD "FRIEND" COME OUT OF SHINOBU'S OWN MOUTH!
BUT...
...I HAD A FLASH OF INSPIRATION.
IN THE 16 YEARS I'VE KNOWN HIM, I'VE NEVER HEARD HIM USE THE WORD "FRIEND."
FOR HIM TO USE IT NOW...
IN OTHER WORDS, WHAT YOU ARE TO HIM...
...OVER THE COURSE OF HIS ENTIRE LIFE...
...HIS VERY FIRST WEAKNESS I COULD GET MY HANDS ON!
AND THAT'S WHEN I CAME UP WITH MY PLAN.
WITH YOU AS MY HOSTAGE, HE CANNOT OPPOSE ME NOW!
HA!
I CAN MAKE ANY DEMAND I WANT, AND HE'LL JUST HAVE TO EAT IT!!
HO HO HO HO HO HO HO HO!!

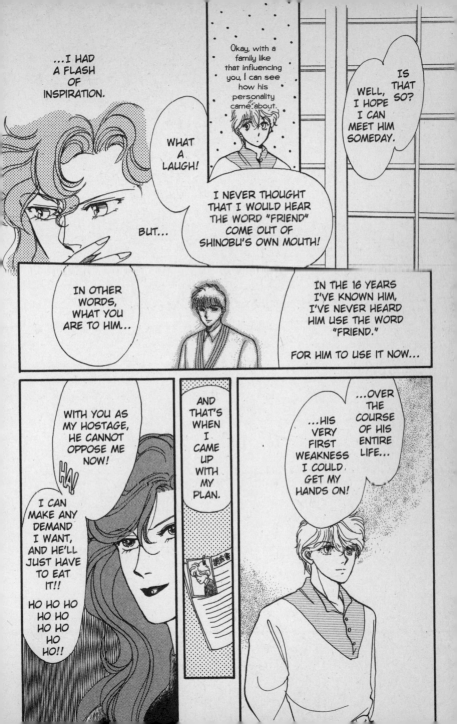

MY YEARS OF LABOR ALL CULMINATE ON THIS DAY!!
SO, WHAT ARE YOU SAYING?
THAT I'M JUST PAYBACK IN SOME CHEAP SIBLING RIVALRY?
"REVENGE"! CALL IT "REVENGE"!!
THERE IS A DIFFERENCE BETWEEN THE DEPTHS OF HATRED AND SOME SIMPLE "RIVALRY"!
YOU ARE A PRISONER OF WAR FOR A SHORT TIME! IF HE MAKES A SMALL APOLOGY TO ME—AND BOWS AND SHOWS ME THE SLIGHTEST BIT OF DEFERENCE—THEN I INTEND TO LET YOU GO UNHARMED.
SO YOUR FUTURE ...
... DEPENDS ON SHINOBU'S ATTITUDE.
I ANTICIPATE GREAT THINGS FROM YOUR "FRIEND."

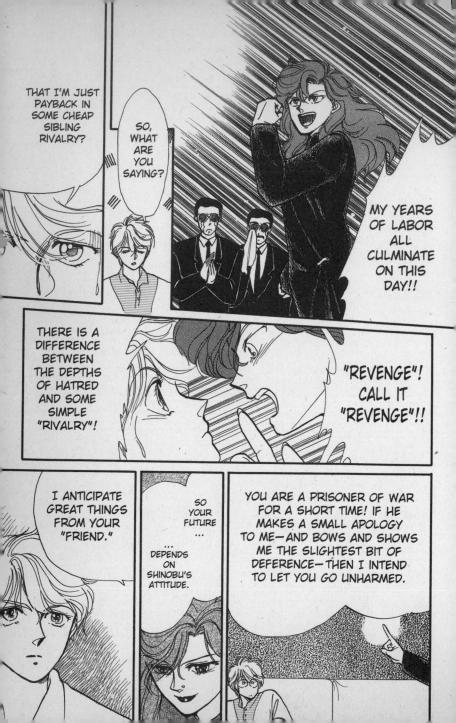

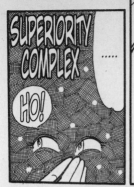

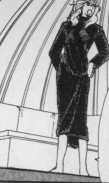

AND HE'S LATE!!
WHY HAVEN'T WE HEARD FROM HIM YET? I WANTED TO TEASE HIM A LITTLE, SO I DIDN'T CONTACT HIM...
...BUT I NEVER EXPECTED HIM TO BE SO DENSE AS TO NOT HAVE FIGURED IT OUT BY NOW!
.....
SUPERIORITY COMPLEX
HO!
ALL RIGHT, FINE!
IF THAT'S THE CASE, WE'LL JUST LET HIM KNOW OURSELVES!
HAND ME THE PHONE!
YES, MA'AM!
SHE AND HASUKAWA MIGHT FIND THEIR OPINIONS ARE PRETTY SIMILAR.
DING-DING-DONNNG
MR. TEZUKA OF ROOM 211, THERE IS A PHONE CALL FOR YOU.
TMP TMP
TMP TMP TMP TMP TMP TMP TMP

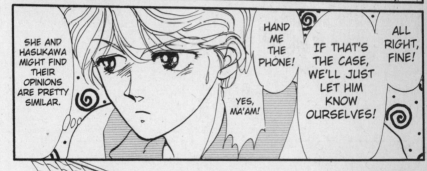

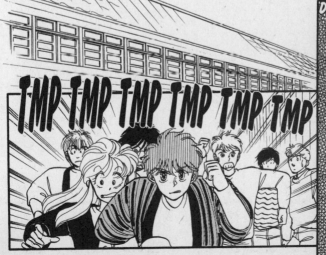

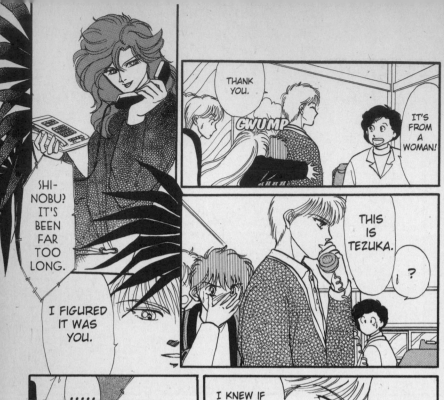

IT'S FROM A WOMAN!
THANK YOU.
GWUMP
THIS IS TEZUKA.
?
SHI-NOBU? IT'S BEEN FAR TOO LONG.
I FIGURED IT WAS YOU.
YOU NEVER DID HAVE ANY PATIENCE, DID YOU?
I KNEW IF I WAITED, YOU WOULD CALL TO LET ME KNOW YOUR PRESENT LOCATION.
YOU'RE THE ONLY ONE IN THE WORLD WHO WOULD RESORT TO KIDNAPPING BECAUSE OF A SIBLING RIVALRY.
.....
IF YOU ALREADY KNOW, THEN I CAN OMIT UNNECESSARY EXPLANATIONS. IF YOU WANT YOUR FRIEND RETURNED UNHARMED, YOU WILL COME HERE IMMEDIATELY! THE ADDRESS IS...
HASU-KAWA, YOUR HAND, PLEASE?
YES?
YOU RENTED ANOTHER APART-MENT?
.....

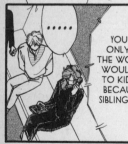

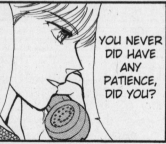

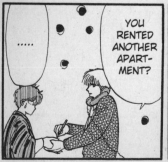

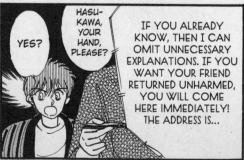

YOU CAN KEEP HIM FOR TWO OR THREE DAYS IF YOU LIKE.
HE SLEEPS ON TOP OF ME AND SNORES SO LOUD, I HAVEN'T HAD A DECENT NIGHT'S SLEEP IN MONTHS.
SHINOBU-SEMPAI!!
AT LEAST MENTION THAT THE DORM HAS BUNK BEDS!
WHO KNOWS HOW THAT STATEMENT COULD BE TAKEN?!
YOU, STAY QUIET!!
HEH
VERY WELL, THEN.
IT SEEMS THAT YOU ALREADY KNOW WHAT I WANT TO SAY.
IF YOU ARE NOT HERE VERY QUICKLY, I CANNOT GUARANTEE YOUR FRIEND'S HEALTH. YOU KNOW THE THINGS I CAN DO IN ORDER TO SEE YOU SUFFER.
OF COURSE, IF HE'S THAT BAD, YOU NEEDN'T COME AT ALL. HOWEVER...
...JUST CONSIDER WHAT THE BOY WILL THINK OF YOU AFTER-WARDS.
I'LL SAY GOODBYE NOW.
I'LL BE WAITING, SHINOBU! ♡
KLIK
KACHAK
THEN WE KNOW WHERE HE'S BEING HELD?
WE HAVE TO GO THERE NOW, SEMPAI!

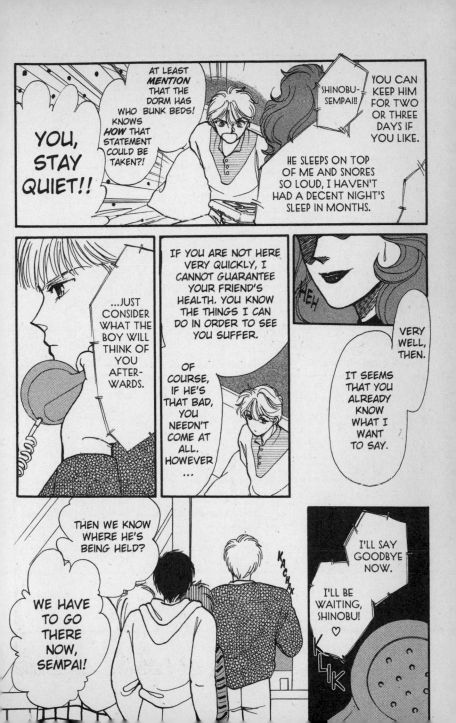

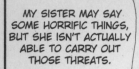

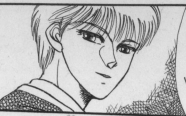

THERE'S NO REASON TO RUSH. HE SOUNDED VERY HEALTHY.
MY SISTER MAY SAY SOME HORRIFIC THINGS, BUT SHE ISN'T ACTUALLY ABLE TO CARRY OUT THOSE THREATS.
SHE IS SO MUCH TROUBLE!
THAT ISN'T THE *POINT* !!
I THOUGHT YOU WERE BETTER THAN THIS!
HOLD IT, SUKA-CHAN, YOU DON'T...
THEY SAY YOU'RE COLD-HEARTED AND THAT NOTHING MOVES YOU, BUT I THOUGHT THAT DEEP INSIDE, YOU WERE WORRIED! BUT NOW...
HASUKAWA, YOU'VE GOT IT ALL WRONG!
SHINOBU IS ACTUALLY NOTHING LIKE THAT!
HE REALLY *IS* COLD-HEARTED.
GUYS, GUYS...
WHEN ARE YOU GOING TO ACCEPT THE FACT THAT *YOU'RE* THE ENTIRE REASON THAT HE WAS KIDNAPPED?!

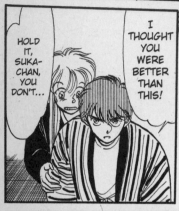

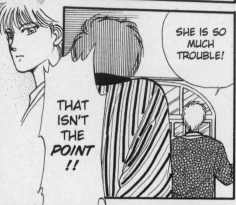

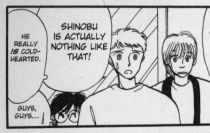

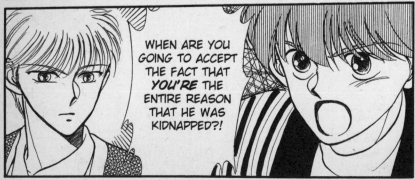

SUKA-CHAN!
EVEN IF YOUR SISTER ISN'T CAPABLE OF HURTING HIM...
...MITSURU BEING THE WAY HE IS, HE MAY JUST BRING SOME CONDITIONS DOWN UPON HIMSELF!
WHAT KIND OF APOLOGY ARE YOU PLANNING TO GIVE HIM THEN?
I CAN SEE THAT HAP-PENING.
HE'S ALWAYS BEEN TOO COCKY.
IF ANYTHING HAPPENS TO MITSURU, I'LL...
HE'S ALREADY BEGINNING TO THINK TWICE ABOUT THE WORDS HE JUST SAID.
HUSSSSSH
TRMBL TRMBL
YOU WISH YOU HADN'T SAID THAT, DON'T YOU?
I-I DO NOT!
I IMAGINE IF HE HEARD THOSE WORDS, HE'D CRY TEARS OF JOY.
ANYWAY, YOU'RE GOING TO HELP ME.

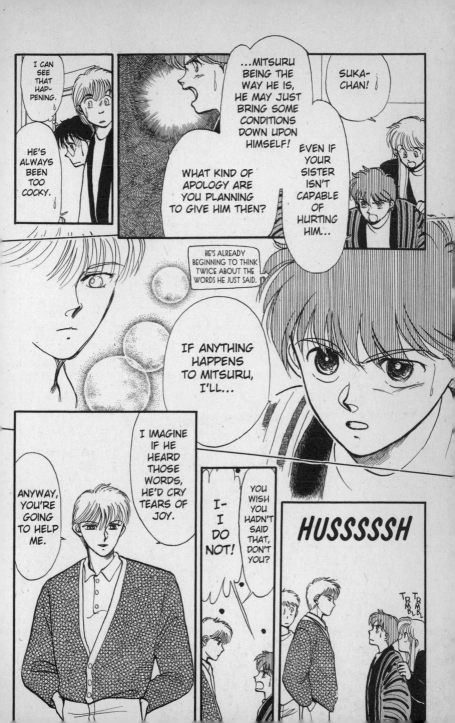

HASUKAWA, SHUN, COME WITH ME.
ALL RIGHT.
HUH?
AND BRING MONEY.
WE'LL HAVE TO TAKE A TAXI.
AND WE'LL HAVE TO TRANSFER BETWEEN THREE TRAIN LINES, I IMAGINE.
WHAT'LL YOU DO? IT'S ALMOST CURFEW.
I'LL HAVE TO LEAVE THOSE DETAILS TO YOU.
I'LL TRY TO HAVE HIM BACK BEFORE LIGHTS-OUT.
OKAY!
I'LL NEED AN ABSENCE SLIP!
IDIOT! NOBODY WILL SIGN IT THIS LATE AT NIGHT!
GOOD LUCK, GUYS!!
MITSURU!
YOU CAN STEAL MY FOOD AND TORTURE ME! JUST BE OKAY!

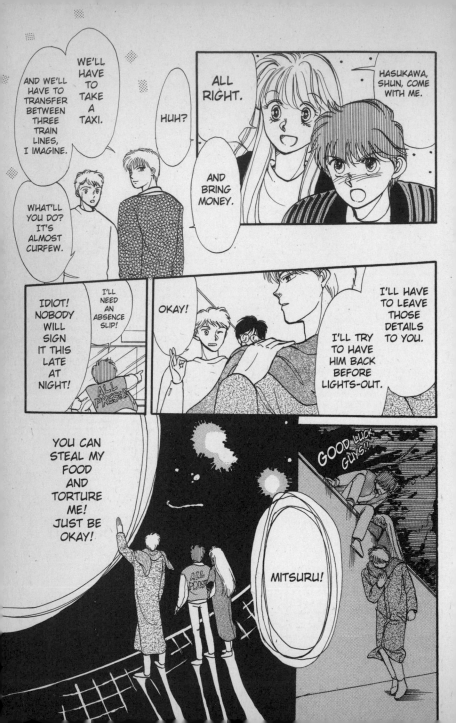

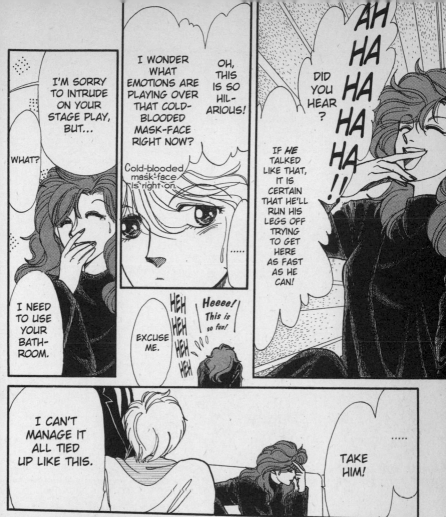

AH HA HA HA HA HA!!
DID YOU HEAR?
IF *HE* TALKED LIKE THAT, IT IS CERTAIN THAT HE'LL RUN HIS LEGS OFF TRYING TO GET HERE AS FAST AS HE CAN!
OH, THIS IS SO HIL-ARIOUS!
I WONDER WHAT EMOTIONS ARE PLAYING OVER THAT COLD-BLOODED MASK-FACE RIGHT NOW?
Cold-blooded mask-face is right on.
.....
I'M SORRY TO INTRUDE ON YOUR STAGE PLAY, BUT...
WHAT?
I NEED TO USE YOUR BATHROOM.
Heeee! This is so fun!
HEH HEH HEH HEH
EXCUSE ME.
.....
TAKE HIM!
I CAN'T MANAGE IT ALL TIED UP LIKE THIS.
COULD YOU...
...MAYBE TIE MY HANDS IN THE FRONT?
MY MUSCLES ARE PRETTY SORE—
YOU'RE PRETTY WHINEY FOR A *HOSTAGE* !!

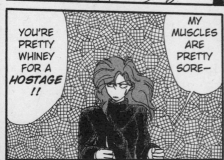

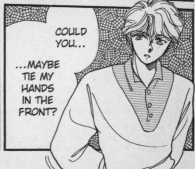

WITH ALL THE GUYS YOU HAVE STANDING GUARD OVER ME, HOW YOU TIE MY HANDS SHOULDN'T BE SUCH A BIG DEAL.
OR MAYBE YOU COULD HELP ME GO. WOULD YOU, MA'AM?
I THINK I'D RATHER DIE THAN HAVE A MAN HELP OUT.
HEY, I'M NOT THRILLED WITH THE IDEA MYSELF!
WHAT SHOULD WE DO?
WE DON'T HAVE MUCH CHOICE.
HOLD STILL.
YUP.
HEY!
GRMP
?!
WAAA!!
HUP

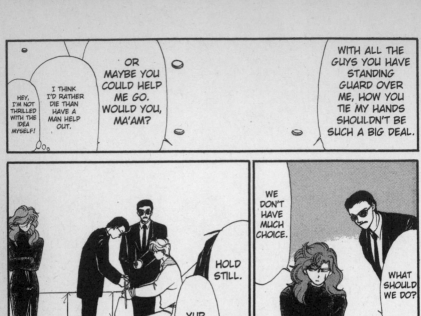

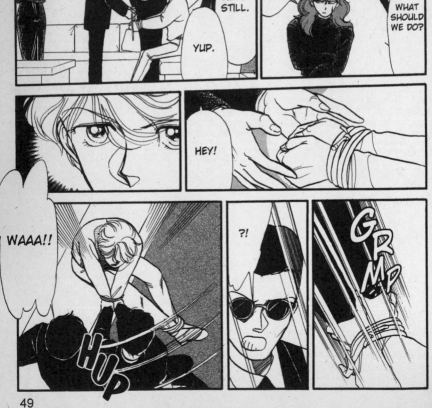

!
DOOMPH
LITTLE PUNK!!
OW.
WHUMP★
TSK!
HEY'RE ETTER HAN I OUGHT !
WHAT DO I DO NOW?
YOU REALLY ARE A LITTLE FOOL!
HOW COULD YOU EXPECT TO ESCAPE FROM A SITUATION LIKE THIS?
H-HE SCARED ME!
I DIDN'T KNOW IF I COULD! I JUST HAD TO TRY TO ESCAPE ON MY OWN.
WHO KNOWS WHAT SHINOBU WILL SAY WHEN HE COMES?
HE'S SO PREDICTABLE!

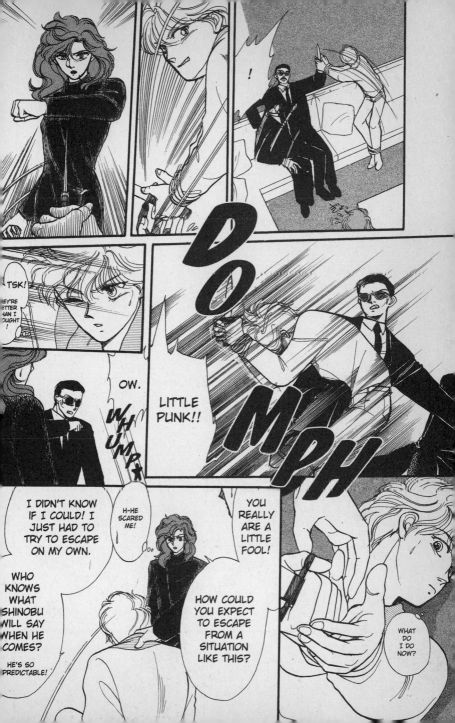

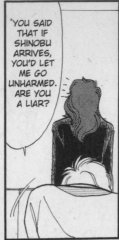

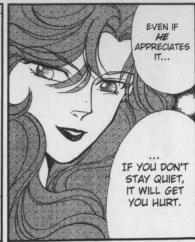

EVEN IF *HE* APPRECIATES IT...
... IF YOU DON'T STAY QUIET, IT WILL GET YOU HURT.
YOU SAID THAT IF SHINOBU ARRIVES, YOU'D LET ME GO UNHARMED. ARE YOU A LIAR?
COME NOW.
I SAID THAT I *INTEND* TO LET YOU GO UN-HARMED.
HMM?
I FORGOT TO MENTION IT, BUT WHILE STUDYING YOUR PICTURES AND ADDRESS...
...I FOUND OUT SOMETHING ABOUT YOU THAT RAISED MY IRE.
YOUR IRE?
DID I DO SOME-THING TO OFFEND YOU?

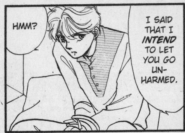

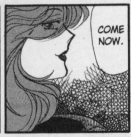

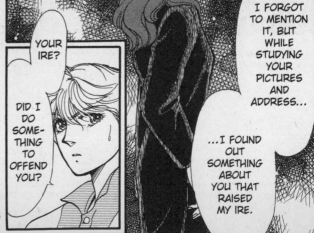

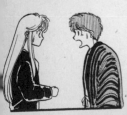

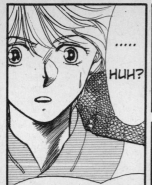

YOU AND I HAVE MET ONCE BEFORE. DON'T YOU REMEMBER?
I'M NOT TALKING ABOUT TODAY.
HA HA HA HA...
.....
HUH?
YOU BEEN TO THE HAGO SHOPPING DISTRICT IN ASAKUSA?
I GUESS...
IT'S NEAR MY HOUSE.
HAS AN UNKNOWN WOMAN EVER TALKED TO YOU THERE?
AND YOU RECEIVED A SHOTOKU-TAISHI 10,000 YEN NOTE* FROM THAT WOMAN.
YOU TOOK THE WOMAN'S HAND AND WALKED WITH HER AS IF YOU WERE HER FRIEND...
THEN, LOOKING AT THE WOMAN AND ALMOST READING THE DISORIENTATION IN HER MIND, YOU TOOK HER HAND...
...AND LED HER IN AND AMONGST THE BUSTLING CROWED STREETS...
...AND WHEN YOU SAW YOUR CHANCE, YOU DISAPPEARED AND ESCAPED.
AHH!
OH, YEAH! THAT'S JUST HOW IT HAPPENED!
AND RIGHT AFTER THAT, I RAN HOME...
YOU CAN'T BE...
YOU FINALLY REMEMBER!

*WENT OUT OF CIRCULATION IN 1984.

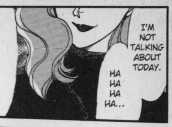

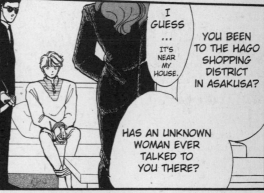

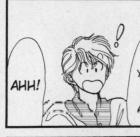

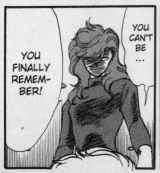

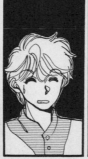

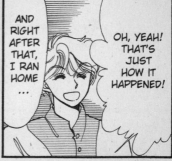

AS I LOOKED AT YOUR PICTURES, I COULDN'T SHAKE THE FEELING THAT I HAD SEEN YOU SOME-WHERE BEFORE.
AND YOUR FACE ...
...NEVER LEFT MY MIND FOR A SINGLE DAY SINCE THEN!
YOU'RE KIDDING!
IT HAPPENED FIVE WHOLE YEARS AGO!!
AWWW! NO MATTER HOW I THINK OF IT, ¥10,000* WAS TOO CHEAP A PRICE!
SHUT YOUR MOUTH!!
I DON'T CARE HOW MANY YEARS IT TAKES! I GET PAYBACK MANY TIMES OVER FOR THE HUMIL-IATIONS I SUFFER!!
THAT IS HOW THE TEZUKA FAMILY WORKS!!
I WILL TAKE THE MEASURE OF THAT ¥10,000 BACK FROM YOU, PLUS SEVERAL YEARS' INTEREST!!
HO HO HO HO HO
HO HO HO HO HO HO HO
IS THIS MISTRESS OF YOURS ALWAYS LIKE THIS?
SHE'S ALSO KNOWN AS THE QUEEN OF HEARTS, AND SOME CALL HER SISTER JILL.*
THANKS.

Ed Note: *About $100.

*The nemesis of Cutie Honey.

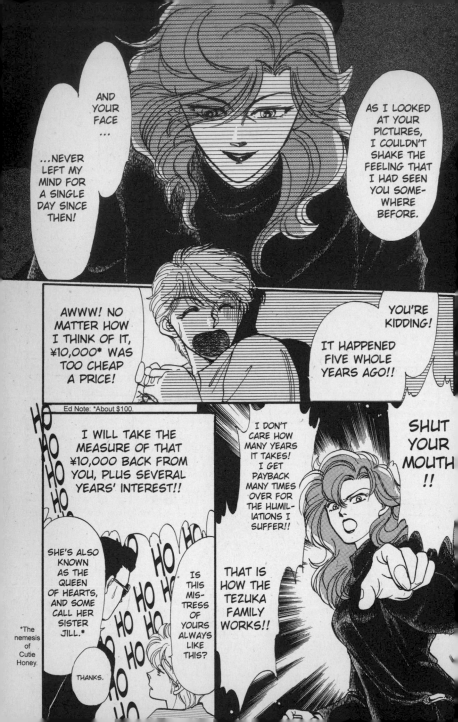

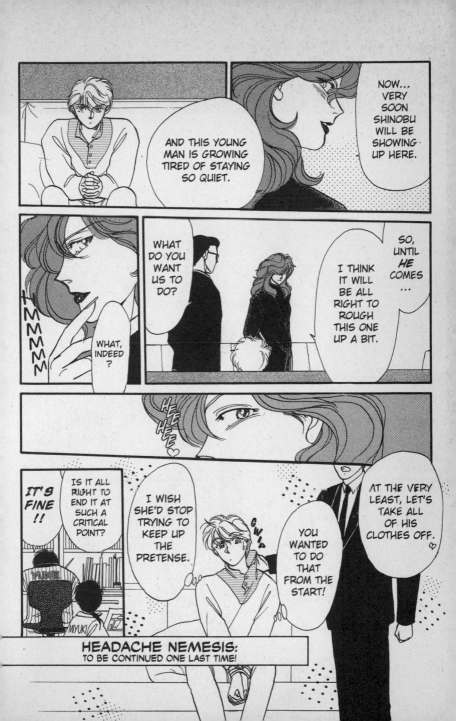

NOW... VERY SOON SHINOBU WILL BE SHOWING UP HERE.
AND THIS YOUNG MAN IS GROWING TIRED OF STAYING SO QUIET.
SO, UNTIL *HE* COMES...
I THINK IT WILL BE ALL RIGHT TO ROUGH THIS ONE UP A BIT.
WHAT DO YOU WANT US TO DO?
HMMMMM
WHAT, INDEED?
HEE HEE HEE♡
AT THE VERY LEAST, LET'S TAKE ALL OF HIS CLOTHES OFF.♡
YOU WANTED TO DO THAT FROM THE START!
GWIP
I WISH SHE'D STOP TRYING TO KEEP UP THE PRETENSE.
IS IT ALL RIGHT TO END IT AT SUCH A CRITICAL POINT?
IT'S FINE!!
YUKIE
MIYUKI
HEADACHE NEMESIS:
TO BE CONTINUED ONE LAST TIME!

EMINI
YCLI
THE

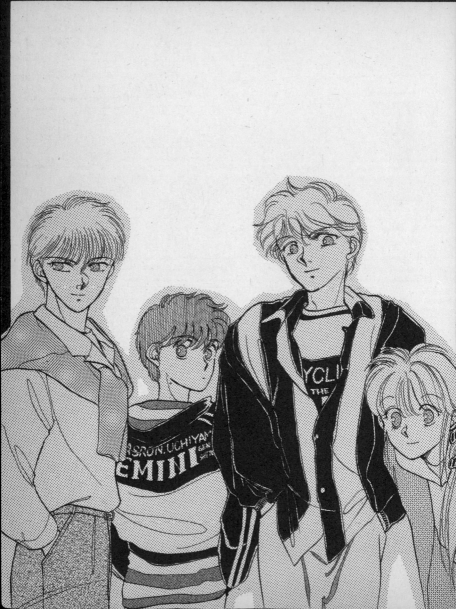

IN USE
SUKA-CHAN?
HUH?
I'M SORRY I LASHED OUT AT YOU THIS AFTERNOON.
I GUESS EVEN *YOU* LIKE MITSURU.
I *CAN* BE A LITTLE COLD SOMETIMES.

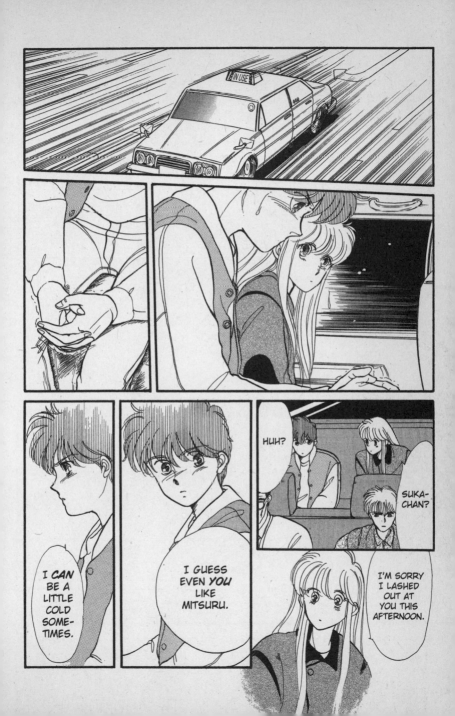

I'M SURE MITSURU IS OKAY!
WE'LL GET HIM HOME ALL RIGHT!
YEAH, KNOWING HIM...
...HE WOULDN'T DIE EVEN IF THEY TRIED TO MURDER HIM.
BUT IF ANYTHING HAPPENS TO HIM...
MAKE A LEFT HERE.
...I'LL MAKE SURE SHINOBU AND HIS SISTER...
...NEVER REST EASY AGAIN!
HERE?
YES.
THE TOP-FLOOR APARTMENT OF THIS BUILDING.
HUH?
SHI-NOBU, WHERE ARE YOU GOING?
FIRST, I HAVE TO MAKE A STOP AT THE PARKING LOT.
SHINOBU!!
AWW, MAN!!

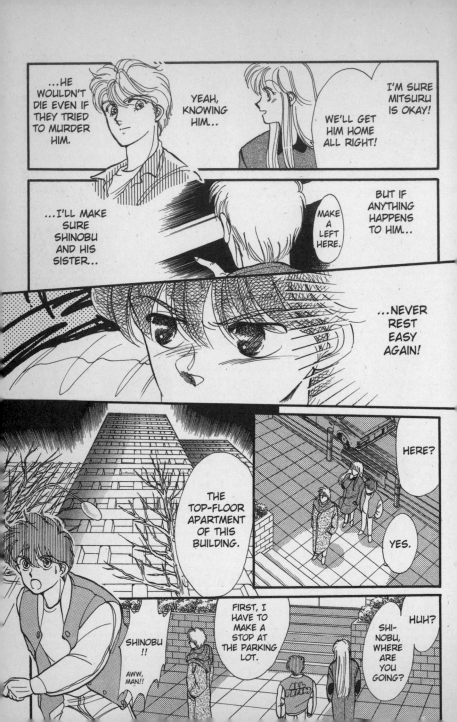

IS THIS IT, SHUN?
YEAH, I'M SURE OF IT.
SO THAT MEANS THAT MITSURU IS HERE FOR SURE, RIGHT?
IT SURE SEEMS THAT WAY.
FWH
SKEE
SKEEEEEEECH

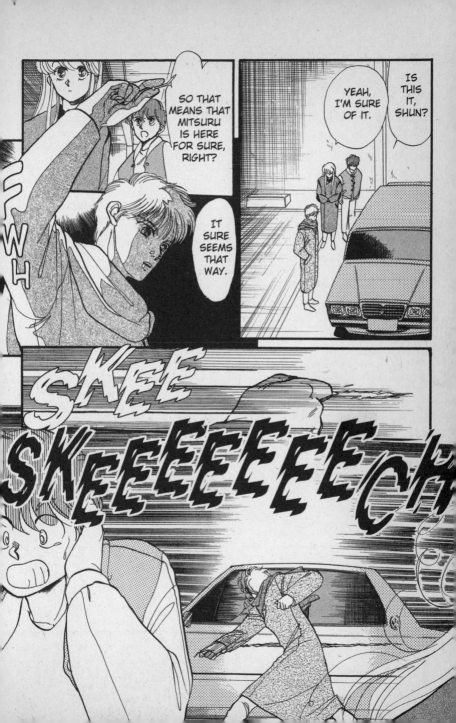

EYUUUU!
LET'S GO.
TAK
TAK TAK
HEY, SUKA-CHAN... YOU DON'T THINK...
...THAT EVER SINCE THIS AFTER-NOON...
...DEEP DOWN, SHINOBU'S BEEN REALLY, REALLY ANGRY?
TAK
I DON'T KNOW...
TAK TAK
TAK
I MUST SAY...
...YOU HAVE GUTS, YOUNG MAN.
I TOLD YOU I WAS HUNGRY.
CHOMP

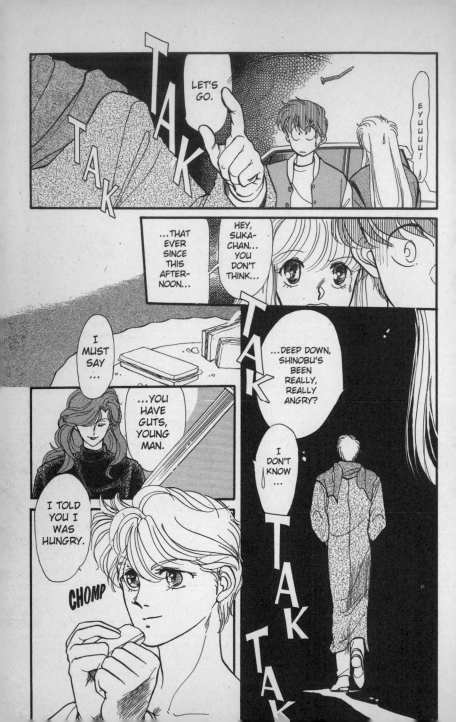

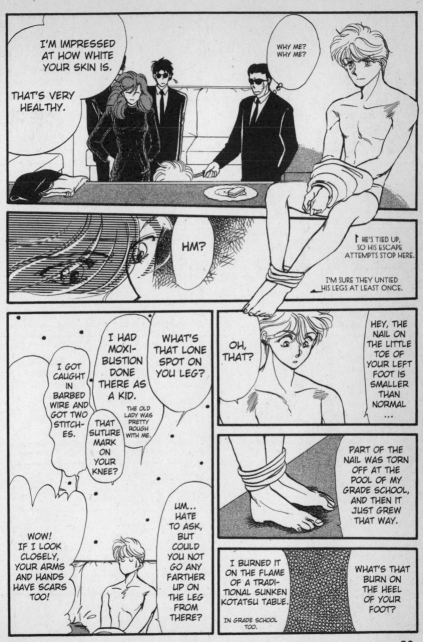

WHY ME? WHY ME?
I'M IMPRESSED AT HOW WHITE YOUR SKIN IS.
THAT'S VERY HEALTHY.
HE'S TIED UP, SO HIS ESCAPE ATTEMPTS STOP HERE.
I'M SURE THEY UNTIED HIS LEGS AT LEAST ONCE.
HM?
HEY, THE NAIL ON THE LITTLE TOE OF YOUR LEFT FOOT IS SMALLER THAN NORMAL ...
OH, THAT?
PART OF THE NAIL WAS TORN OFF AT THE POOL OF MY GRADE SCHOOL, AND THEN IT JUST GREW THAT WAY.
WHAT'S THAT BURN ON THE HEEL OF YOUR FOOT?
I BURNED IT ON THE FLAME OF A TRADI-TIONAL SUNKEN KOTATSU TABLE.
IN GRADE SCHOOL TOO.
WHAT'S THAT LONE SPOT ON YOU LEG?
I HAD MOXI-BUSTION DONE THERE AS A KID.
THE OLD LADY WAS PRETTY ROUGH WITH ME.
THAT SUTURE MARK ON YOUR KNEE?
I GOT CAUGHT IN BARBED WIRE AND GOT TWO STITCH-ES.
UM... HATE TO ASK, BUT COULD YOU NOT GO ANY FARTHER UP ON THE LEG FROM THERE?
WOW! IF I LOOK CLOSELY, YOUR ARMS AND HANDS HAVE SCARS TOO!

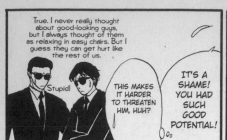

YOUR BODY IS A TESTAMENT TO YOUR UPBRINGING, HMM?
THEY'RE MEDALS OF HONOR.
IT'S A SHAME! YOU HAD SUCH GOOD POTENTIAL!
THIS MAKES IT HARDER TO THREATEN HIM, HUH?
Stupid!
True. I never really thought about good-looking guys, but I always thought of them as relaxing in easy chairs. But I guess they can get hurt like the rest of us.
ACTUALLY ...
...THE FIRST TIME I HEARD ABOUT YOU, IT STRUCK ME AS ODD.
WHY WOULD THE FIRST PERSON THAT SHINOBU EVER ALLOWED HIMSELF TO BE BOUND TO BE A...A NOBODY OF SUCH QUESTIONABLE BACKGROUND?
I MEAN, IT WOULD DO NOTHING FOR THAT BOY TO WIN YOUR FAVOR.
SO YOU CONSIDER FRIENDSHIP TO BE SOME KIND OF "BIND"?
Ack! They put too much hot sauce in this.
HE LOOKS AT IT THAT WAY.
HE'S NEVER SEEN ANYTHING OR ANYONE AS EXISTING AT THE SAME LEVEL AS HIMSELF.
PEOPLE DON'T ALWAYS STAY THE WAY THEY ARE.

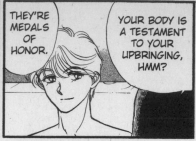

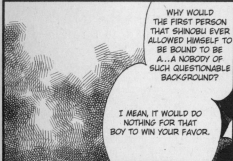

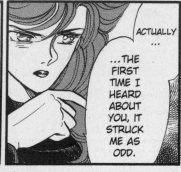

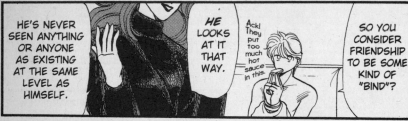

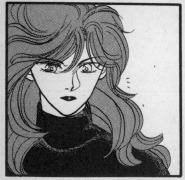

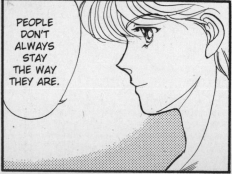

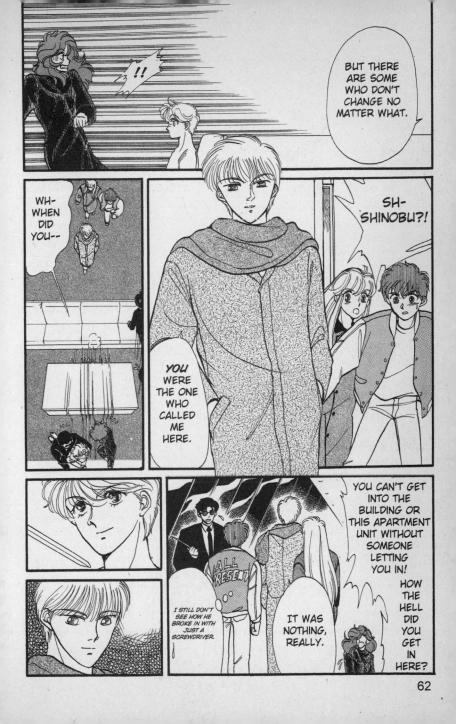

!!
BUT THERE ARE SOME WHO DON'T CHANGE NO MATTER WHAT.
SH- SHINOBU?!
WH- WHEN DID YOU--
YOU WERE THE ONE WHO CALLED ME HERE.
YOU CAN'T GET INTO THE BUILDING OR THIS APARTMENT UNIT WITHOUT SOMEONE LETTING YOU IN!
HOW THE HELL DID YOU GET IN HERE?
IT WAS NOTHING, REALLY.
I STILL DON'T SEE HOW HE BROKE IN WITH JUST A SCREWDRIVER.
ALL PRESENT

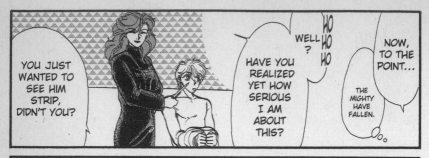

NOW, TO THE POINT...
THE MIGHTY HAVE FALLEN.
HO HO HO
WELL?
HAVE YOU REALIZED YET HOW SERIOUS I AM ABOUT THIS?
YOU JUST WANTED TO SEE HIM STRIP, DIDN'T YOU?
YOU HAVEN'T GAINED EVEN THE *LITTLEST* BIT OF TACT, HAVE YOU?!
SHINOBU! WHAT GOOD DOES IT DO TO PROVOKE HER NOW?!
I DON'T CARE WHAT KIND OF ANGELIC FACE YOU PUT ON—IT WON'T SWAY ME!
I SEE YOU'VE BROUGHT ALONG YOUR UNDERLINGS. WELCOME, LITTLE BOYS.
THIS WILL SOON BE OVER, SO STAY STILL AND LEARN.
YOU'VE PUT YOUR OLDER SISTER THROUGH A LOT OF GRIEF FOR A LONG TIME, SHINOBU.
YOU PUT YOUR-SELF THROUGH IT.
IF YOU OPEN THAT FILTHY MOUTH OF YOURS ONE MORE TIME ...
...YOU'LL RISK SCARRING YOUR FRIEND'S FACE FOREVER!!
.....
!!

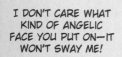

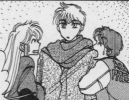

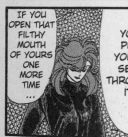

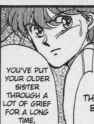

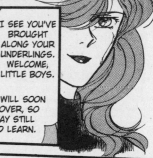

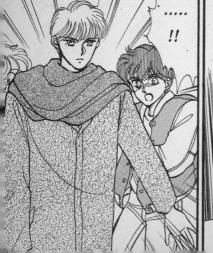

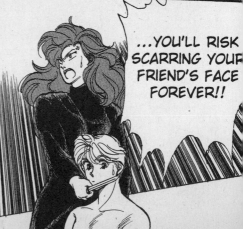

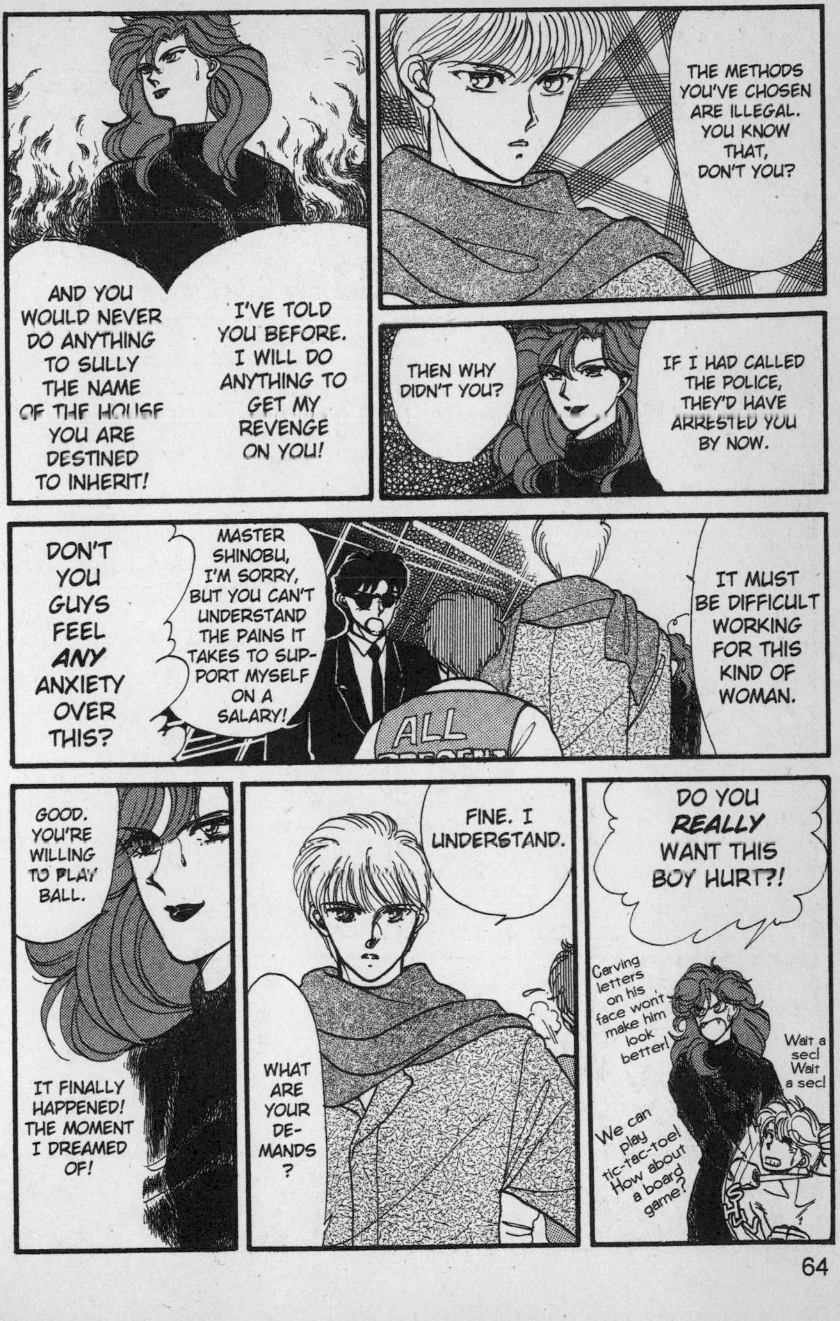
THE METHODS YOU'VE CHOSEN ARE ILLEGAL. YOU KNOW THAT, DON'T YOU?
IF I HAD CALLED THE POLICE, THEY'D HAVE ARRESTED YOU BY NOW.
THEN WHY DIDN'T YOU?
I'VE TOLD YOU BEFORE. I WILL DO ANYTHING TO GET MY REVENGE ON YOU!
AND YOU WOULD NEVER DO ANYTHING TO SULLY THE NAME OF THE HOUSE YOU ARE DESTINED TO INHERIT!
IT MUST BE DIFFICULT WORKING FOR THIS KIND OF WOMAN.
MASTER SHINOBU, I'M SORRY, BUT YOU CAN'T UNDERSTAND THE PAINS IT TAKES TO SUPPORT MYSELF ON A SALARY!
DON'T YOU GUYS FEEL ANY ANXIETY OVER THIS?
ALL
DO YOU REALLY WANT THIS BOY HURT?!
Wait a sec! Wait a sec!
Carving letters on his face won't make him look better!
We can play tic-tac-toe! How about a board game?
FINE. I UNDERSTAND.
WHAT ARE YOUR DEMANDS?
GOOD. YOU'RE WILLING TO PLAY BALL.
IT FINALLY HAPPENED! THE MOMENT I DREAMED OF!

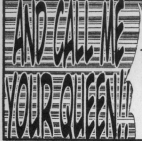

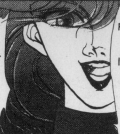

FIRST, TO APOLOGIZE FOR THE COUNTLESS INDIGNITIES I HAD TO SUFFER, I WANT YOU TO GROVEL ON THE GROUND BEFORE ME!
THEN CRAWL TOWARD ME AND KISS MY FEET!
AND CALL ME YOUR QUEEN!!
DAMMIT!
SH-SHE *IS* A DEVIANT!
YOU SHALL KNOW THE BLACK FIRE THAT HAS BURNED HIDDEN BENEATH MY CHEST FOR YEARS ON END!
.....
WELL? WHAT WILL YOU DO NOW, SHINOBU?!
MS. NAGISA?
I HAVE A TALENT: WOULD YOU LIKE TO SEE IT? IT'LL COST YOU ¥10,000, BUT...
WHAT ARE YOU TALKING ABOUT?

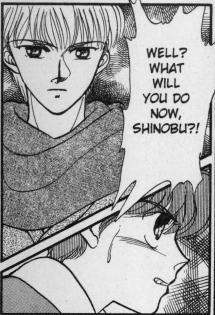

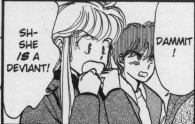

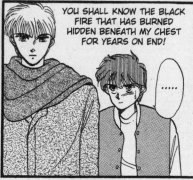

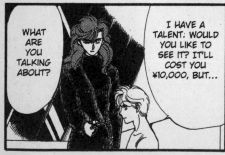

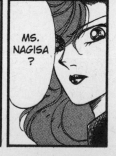

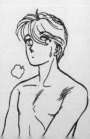

EEEEH?!
HUH?
AS HARD AS HE CAN...
SLISSS
YOU...
WHAT...

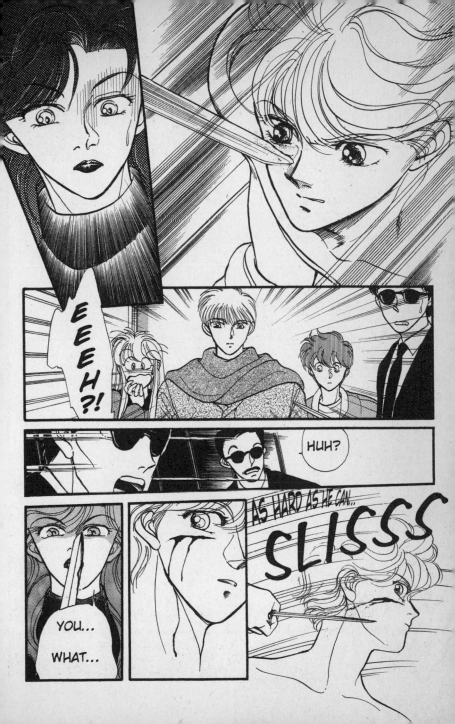

WHAT DO YOU THINK YOU'RE *DOING?!*
FWIP
OH!
SLTZ
PLIP PLIP PLIP
HUH?
WHAT'S HE DOING?
DON'T LET HIM GET AWAY!!
SKREE
KACHK KACHK
WREN-TINK

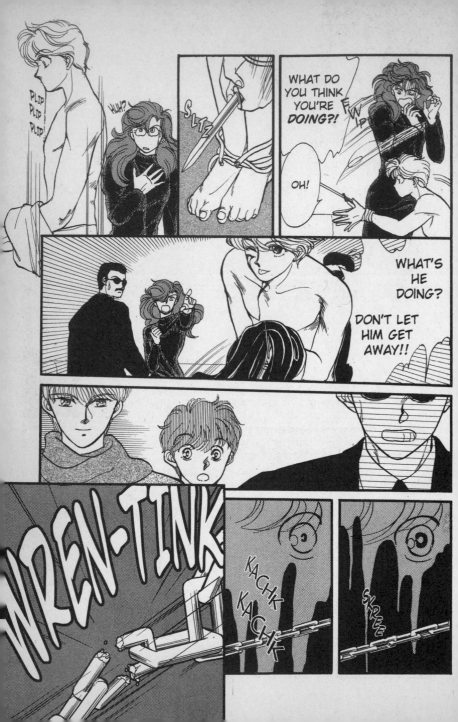

SHK
DAMN ...
YOUUUUUUUUUU!!
AAAAH!
WHAT'S WITH THIS KID?!
DAMMIT! DAMMIT!
YOU CUT UP MITSURU'S FACE!!
WHAT'S YOUR PROBLEM? HE DID IT HIMSELF!!
BAFF
POWW
BAMM
SHINOBU, CUT MY HANDS FREE, WILL YOU?
Oh, geez! Oh, geez!
WE'LL JUST CALL THIS A DEBT.
HASUKAWA, YOU CAN STOP NOW.
BIFF
WHAT ARE YOU TALKING ABOUT? YOUR FACE—
CAN'T BE HELPED, HMM?
DRESSED ALREADY?

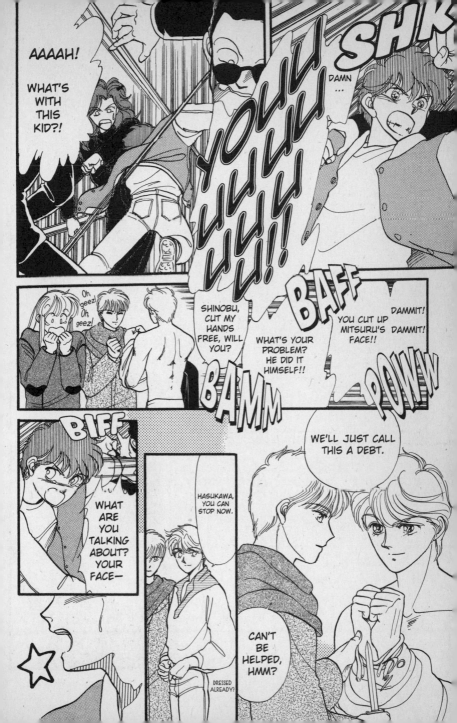

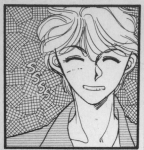
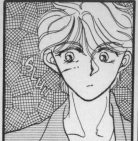
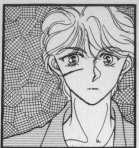

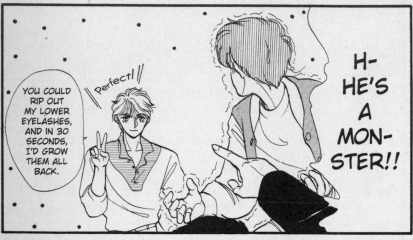

YOU COULD RIP OUT MY LOWER EYELASHES, AND IN 30 SECONDS, I'D GROW THEM ALL BACK.

Perfect!

H-HE'S A MON-STER!!

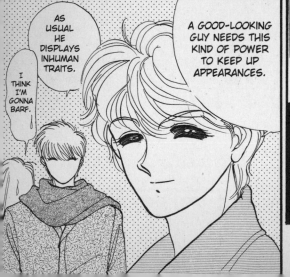

AS USUAL HE DISPLAYS INHUMAN TRAITS.

I THINK I'M GONNA BARF.

A GOOD-LOOKING GUY NEEDS THIS KIND OF POWER TO KEEP UP APPEARANCES.

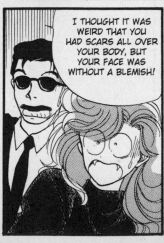

I THOUGHT IT WAS WEIRD THAT YOU HAD SCARS ALL OVER YOUR BODY, BUT YOUR FACE WAS WITHOUT A BLEMISH!

HE-
HUH? HASUKAWA?
HE'S NOT HUMAN!
SLUMP
I KNEW YUKIE NASU COULDN'T WRITE A STORY WITHOUT SOME KIND OF BIZARRE CHARACTER COMING TO LIFE!
Oh, leave me alone!
FLUMP
WHAT'S WRONG? HEY!
IT'S POSSIBLE THAT THEY MIGHT HAVE MURDERED HIM, AND HE WOULDN'T DIE!
I SEE. THIS IS THE REASON THAT SHINOBU WAS SO UNUSUALLY CALM!
DON'T PASS OUT ON US!
HM?
WHAT THE HELL!
HOW AM I SUPPOSED TO WIN AGAINST AN ENEMY LIKE THAT?
HE'S GOT A FEVER.

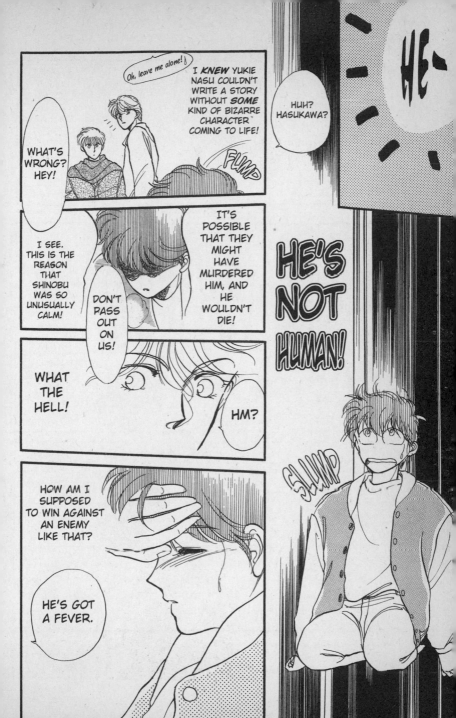

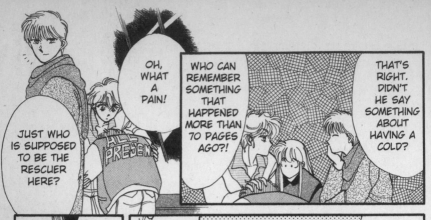

THAT'S RIGHT. DIDN'T HE SAY SOMETHING ABOUT HAVING A COLD?
WHO CAN REMEMBER SOMETHING THAT HAPPENED MORE THAN 70 PAGES AGO?!
OH, WHAT A PAIN!
JUST WHO IS SUPPOSED TO BE THE RESCUER HERE?
NAGISA!
WHUMP
IT'S OKAY, SHI-NOBU.
BUT...
IT'S OKAY.
THERE'S A LOT I CAN SYMPATHIZE WITH THERE.
YOU MADE A LOT OF MIS-LEADING STATE-MENTS ABOUT THINGS SUCH AS OUR HOUSEHOLD.
AND TODAY, I'M GOING TO LET YOU GET AWAY WITH THEM.
I WON'T TELL THE MAIN HOUSE WHAT YOU DID.
JIKK
AND I'LL ASK YOU TO REFRAIN FROM DOING THINGS THAT WILL EMBARRASS YOUR BROTHERS IN ANY WAY. BUT ONE MORE THING...

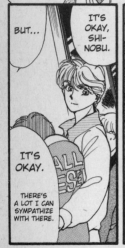

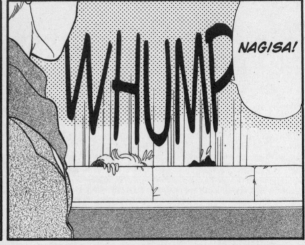

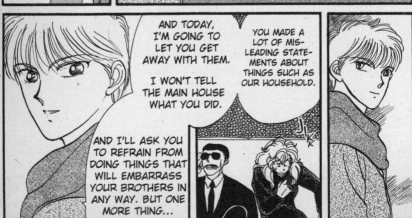

GWAAA
IF BY SOME COSMIC REASON YOU ATTEMPT SOME IDIOTIC ACT LIKE THIS AGAIN...
...I WILL SHOW NO MERCY!!
SHHH—TINK
WELL, THEN...
IT SEEMS YOU WERE LUCKY...
...IN YOUR CHOICE OF PLAYERS THIS TIME.
KRAKK
UNH!
I SEE...
MY PLAN WAS FLAWED.
KRMBL
WHO IS HE? MEDUSA ?
KRMBL

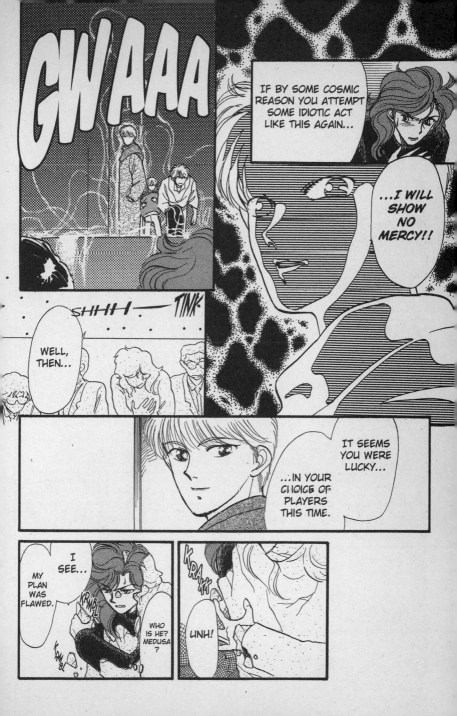

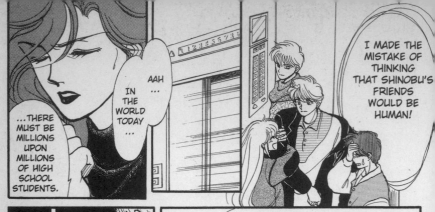

I MADE THE MISTAKE OF THINKING THAT SHINOBU'S FRIENDS WOULD BE HUMAN!
AAH ...
IN THE WORLD TODAY ...
...THERE MUST BE MILLIONS UPON MILLIONS OF HIGH SCHOOL STUDENTS.
WHY IS IT THAT I ALWAYS GET DRAWN TO THIS TYPE?!
AH!
← TOCHIZAWA AND THE GUYS AT THE DORM MUST BE WORRIED!
LET'S GIVE THEM A CALL!
THIS GUY'S ALMOST GONE.
HE'S ABOUT TO COL-LAPSE.

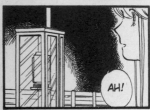

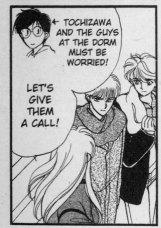

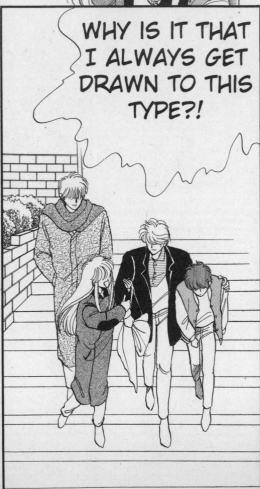

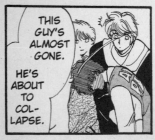

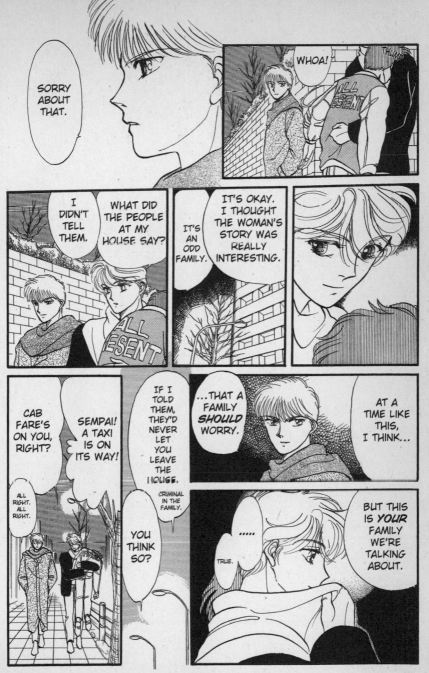

WHOA!
THUMP
SORRY ABOUT THAT.
WHAT DID THE PEOPLE AT MY HOUSE SAY?
I DIDN'T TELL THEM.
IT'S OKAY. I THOUGHT THE WOMAN'S STORY WAS REALLY INTERESTING.
IT'S AN ODD FAMILY.
IF I TOLD THEM, THEY'D NEVER LET YOU LEAVE THE HOUSE.
AT A TIME LIKE THIS, I THINK...
...THAT A FAMILY *SHOULD* WORRY.
BUT THIS IS *YOUR* FAMILY WE'RE TALKING ABOUT.
.....
TRUE.
YOU THINK SO?
CRIMINAL IN THE FAMILY.
SEMPAI! A TAXI IS ON ITS WAY!
CAB FARE'S ON YOU, RIGHT?
ALL RIGHT. ALL RIGHT.

I WAS WONDERING. I CAN UNDERSTAND WHY YOU BROUGHT SHUN ALONG. HE WAS A WITNESS. BUT WHY HASUKAWA?
.....
I HAPPENED TO WRITE THE ADDRESS HERE ON HIS HAND.
REALLY ?
AND SO...
...WHILE I WAS STILL UNCON-SCIOUS...
UMPH! A LITTLE MORE...
...I CAN'T SAY THAT I KNOW WHAT HAPPENED...
I'M SO FRUS-TRATED !!

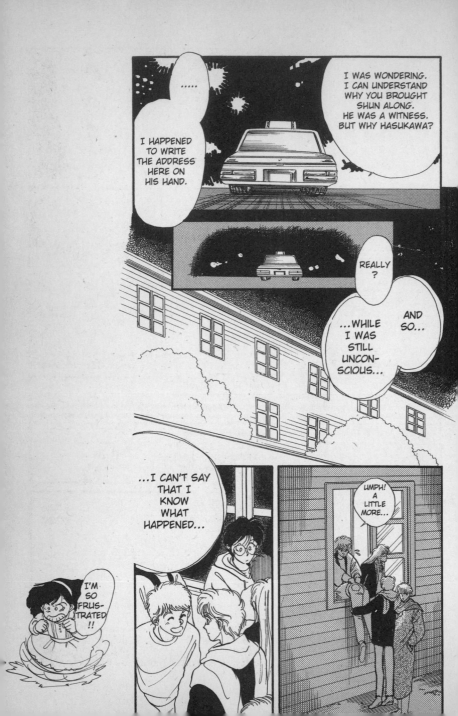

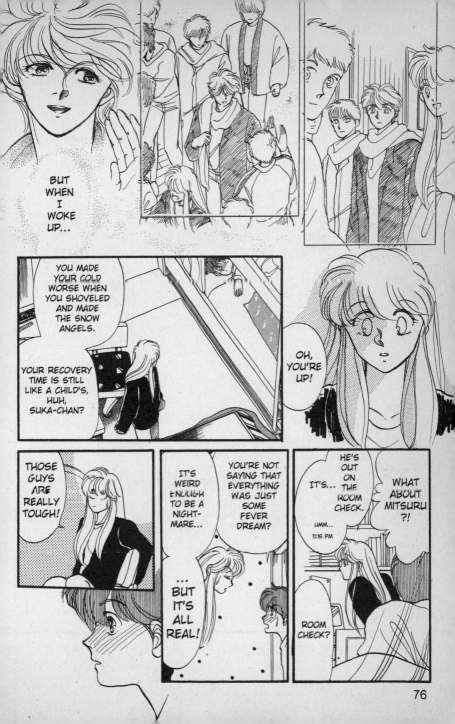

BUT WHEN I WOKE UP...
OH, YOU'RE UP!
YOU MADE YOUR COLD WORSE WHEN YOU SHOVELED AND MADE THE SNOW ANGELS.
YOUR RECOVERY TIME IS STILL LIKE A CHILD'S, HUH, SUKA-CHAN?
WHAT ABOUT MITSURU?!
IT'S... HE'S OUT ON THE ROOM CHECK.
UMM.. 11:15 PM
ROOM CHECK?
YOU'RE NOT SAYING THAT EVERYTHING WAS JUST SOME FEVER DREAM?
IT'S WEIRD ENOUGH TO BE A NIGHTMARE...
...BUT IT'S ALL REAL!
THOSE GUYS ARE REALLY TOUGH!

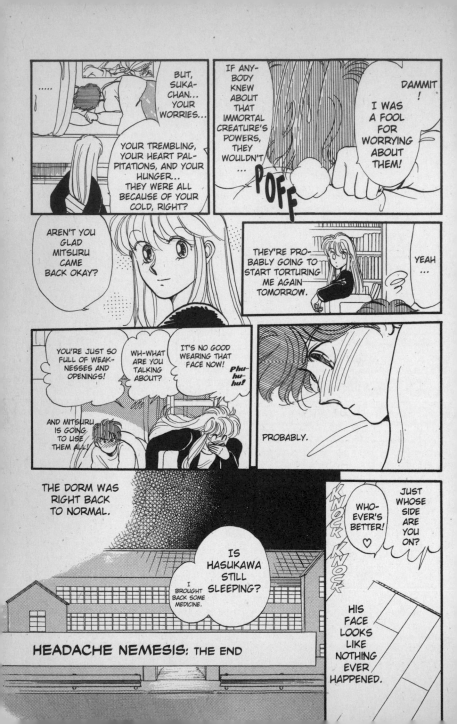

......

BUT, SUKA-CHAN... YOUR WORRIES...

YOUR TREMBLING, YOUR HEART PALPITATIONS, AND YOUR HUNGER... THEY WERE ALL BECAUSE OF YOUR COLD, RIGHT?

IF ANY-BODY KNEW ABOUT THAT IMMORTAL CREATURE'S POWERS, THEY WOULDN'T...

POFF

DAMMIT!

I WAS A FOOL FOR WORRYING ABOUT THEM!

AREN'T YOU GLAD MITSURU CAME BACK OKAY?

THEY'RE PRO-BABLY GOING TO START TORTURING ME AGAIN TOMORROW.

YEAH...

YOU'RE JUST SO FULL OF WEAK-NESSES AND OPENINGS!

WH-WHAT ARE YOU TALKING ABOUT?

IT'S NO GOOD WEARING THAT FACE NOW!

Phu-hu-hu!

AND MITSURU IS GOING TO USE THEM ALL!

PROBABLY.

THE DORM WAS RIGHT BACK TO NORMAL.

IS HASUKAWA STILL SLEEPING?

I BROUGHT BACK SOME MEDICINE.

KNOCK KNOCK

WHO-EVER'S BETTER! ♥

JUST WHOSE SIDE ARE YOU ON?

HIS FACE LOOKS LIKE NOTHING EVER HAPPENED.

HEADACHE NEMESIS: THE END

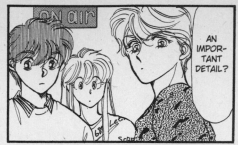

ON AIR
BY THE WAY, THERE'S ONE IMPORTANT DETAIL WE FORGOT.
AN IMPOR-TANT DETAIL?
SHOULDN'T WE BE A YEAR OLDER BY NOW?
HEY!
?
WHAT'S THIS?
IT'S NASU!
I GUESS THAT'S TRUE.
SO THAT MEANS WE'LL NEVER GRADUATE?
HEY! JUST HOLD ON ONE SECOND!!
A GOOD CHARACTER WON'T BRING UP PROBLEMS THAT THE ARTIST ALREADY SUCCESSFULLY AVOIDED FOUR TIMES IN A ROW! YOU IDIOTS!
DON'T THINK THIS IS OVER!
OH, NO, MISS NAGISA! PLEASE DON'T TRY THIS AGAIN!
DON'T THEY SAY, "EAT THE POISON, AND YOU MIGHT AS WELL EAT OTHER STUFF TOO"?
MISS! THAT'S "...MIGHT AS WELL EAT THE PLATE!"
I WISH I HAD BEEN ASSIGNED TO MASTER SHINOBU!
LET'S MEET AGAIN SOME-TIME!

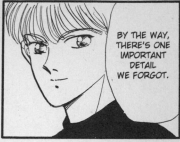

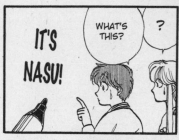

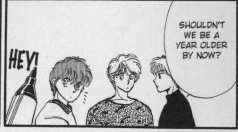

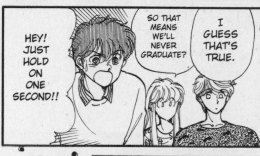

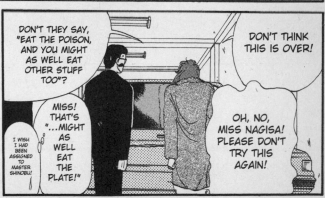

HEADACHE NEMESIS: THE END

BOY
MEETS
BOY

SOUND
MIND
AND
BODY
BOY MEETS BOY

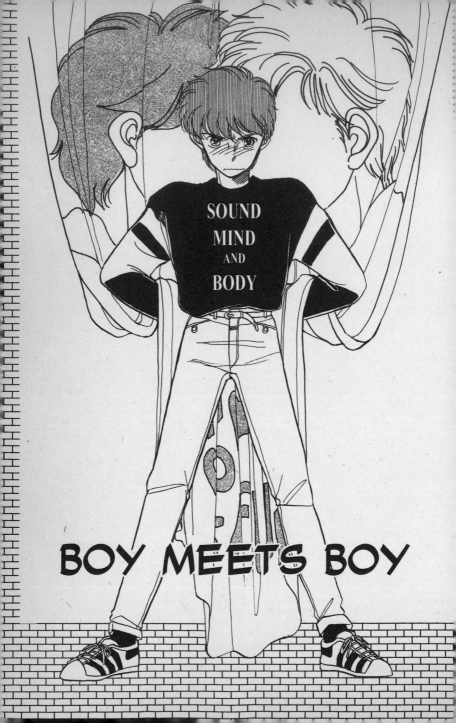

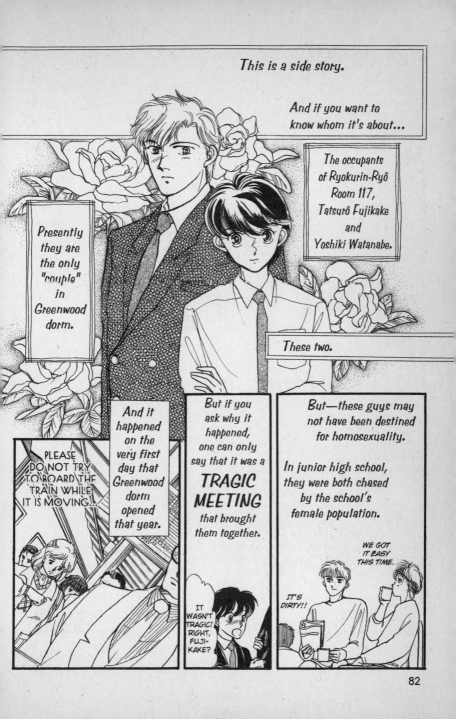

This is a side story.
And if you want to know whom it's about...
The occupants of Ryokurin-Ryô Room 117, Tatsurô Fujikake and Yoshiki Watanabe.
Presently they are the only "couple" in Greenwood dorm.
These two.
And it happened on the very first day that Greenwood dorm opened that year.
PLEASE DO NOT TRY TO BOARD THE TRAIN WHILE IT IS MOVING...
But if you ask why it happened, one can only say that it was a TRAGIC MEETING that brought them together.
IT WASN'T TRAGIC! RIGHT, FUJI-KAKE?
But—these guys may not have been destined for homosexuality.
In junior high school, they were both chased by the school's female population.
WE GOT IT EASY THIS TIME.
IT'S DIRTY!!

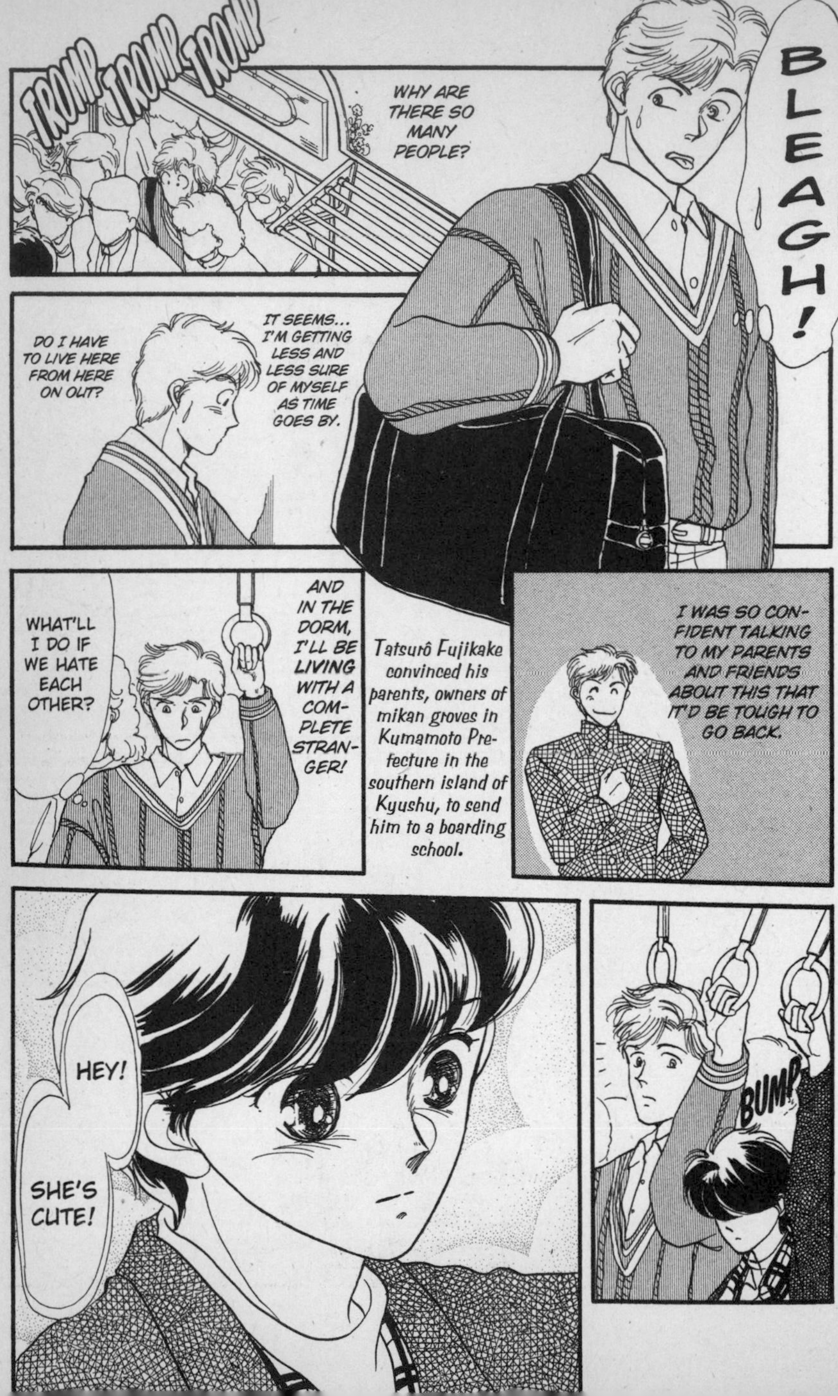

TROMP TROMP TROMP
BLEAGH!
WHY ARE THERE SO MANY PEOPLE?
IT SEEMS... I'M GETTING LESS AND LESS SURE OF MYSELF AS TIME GOES BY.
DO I HAVE TO LIVE HERE FROM HERE ON OUT?
I WAS SO CONFIDENT TALKING TO MY PARENTS AND FRIENDS ABOUT THIS THAT IT'D BE TOUGH TO GO BACK.
Tatsurô Fujikake convinced his parents, owners of mikan groves in Kumamoto Prefecture in the southern island of Kyushu, to send him to a boarding school.
AND IN THE DORM, I'LL BE LIVING WITH A COMPLETE STRANGER!
WHAT'LL I DO IF WE HATE EACH OTHER?
BUMP
HEY!
SHE'S CUTE!

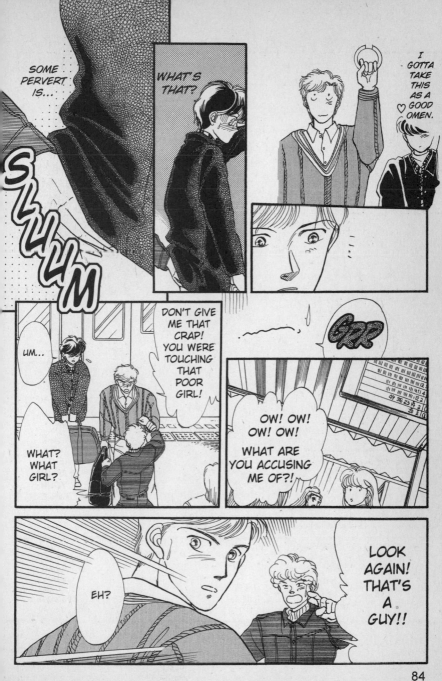

I GOTTA TAKE THIS AS A GOOD OMEN. ♡
WHAT'S THAT?
SOME PERVERT IS...
SLUUM
GRR
OW! OW! OW! OW! WHAT ARE YOU ACCUSING ME OF?!
DON'T GIVE ME THAT CRAP! YOU WERE TOUCHING THAT POOR GIRL!
UM...
WHAT? WHAT GIRL?
LOOK AGAIN! THAT'S A GUY!!
EH?

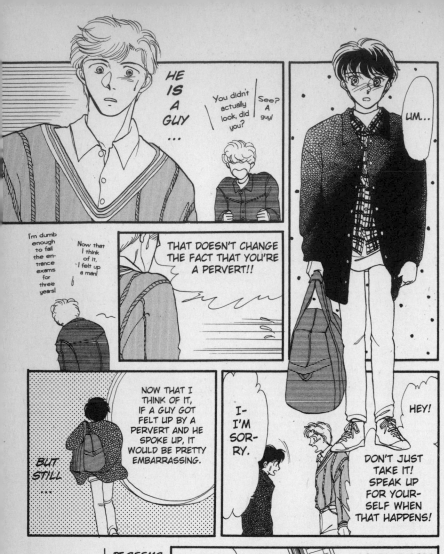

HE IS A GUY...

You didn't actually look, did you?

See? A guy!

UM...

I'm dumb enough to fail the entrance exams for three years!

Now that I think of it, I felt up a man!

THAT DOESN'T CHANGE THE FACT THAT YOU'RE A PERVERT!!

NOW THAT I THINK OF IT, IF A GUY GOT FELT UP BY A PERVERT AND HE SPOKE UP, IT WOULD BE PRETTY EMBARRASSING.

BUT STILL...

I-I'M SOR-RY.

HEY!

DON'T JUST TAKE IT! SPEAK UP FOR YOUR-SELF WHEN THAT HAPPENS!

And thus, the two had their first brush with fate.

IT SEEMS LIKE MY FIRST STEP WAS A REALLY WEIRD ONE.

IT'S TOO BAD. IF HE WERE A GIRL, HE'D BE REALLY CUTE.

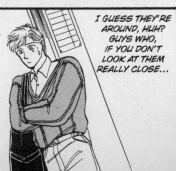

I GUESS THEY'RE AROUND, HUH? GUYS WHO, IF YOU DON'T LOOK AT THEM REALLY CLOSE...

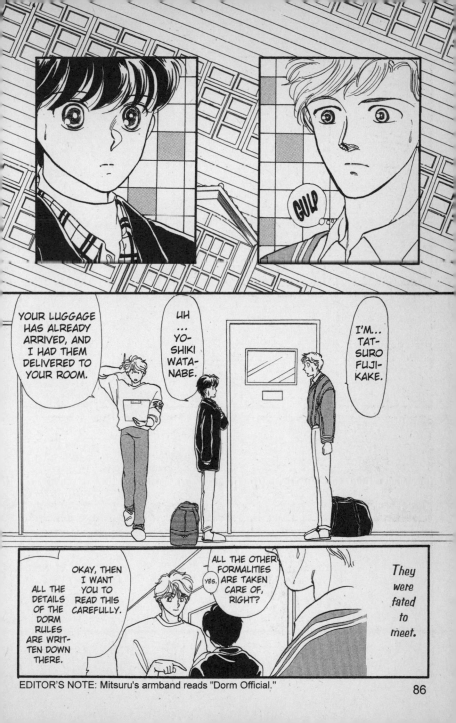

GULP
I'M... TAT-SURO FUJI-KAKE.
UH ... YO-SHIKI WATA-NABE.
YOUR LUGGAGE HAS ALREADY ARRIVED, AND I HAD THEM DELIVERED TO YOUR ROOM.
They were fated to meet.
ALL THE OTHER FORMALITIES ARE TAKEN CARE OF, RIGHT?
YES.
OKAY, THEN I WANT YOU TO READ THIS CAREFULLY.
ALL THE DETAILS OF THE DORM RULES ARE WRIT-TEN DOWN THERE.

EDITOR'S NOTE: Mitsuru's armband reads "Dorm Official."

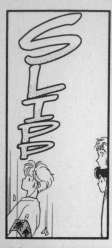

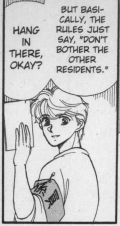

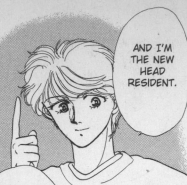

AND I'M THE NEW HEAD RESIDENT.
YOU CAN FIND ME UPSTAIRS IN ROOM 211. IF THERE'S ANYTHING I CAN DO FOR YOU, JUST ASK.
BUT BASICALLY, THE RULES JUST SAY, "DON'T BOTHER THE OTHER RESIDENTS."
HANG IN THERE, OKAY?
SLIPP
.....
YOU'VE BEEN RIDING YOUR MOTORCYCLE IN THE HALLS AGAIN!
FURUSAWA-SEMPAI!!
UH ...
UM ...
YOU A NEW GUY?
YEAH.
KNOW HOW TO PLAY MAH JONG?
MORE OR LESS.
COME WITH ME. WE'RE SHORT ONE GUY.

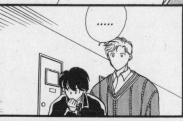

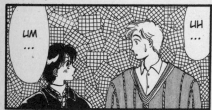

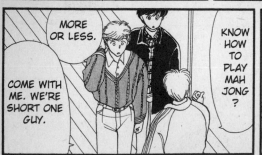

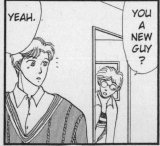

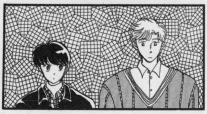

NICE TO MEET YOU.
HEY! NEW GUYS!
EH? OH, YEAH.
SORRY. WE'LL SAVE YOU A SEAT NEXT TIME.
HEY! DON'T HIJACK THE POOR GUYS BEFORE THEY'VE HAD A CHANCE TO PUT THEIR STUFF AWAY!
Run! Run!
ARE YOU NEW? I WAS WONDERING IF YOU WOULD LIKE TO JOIN US IN LISTENING TO THE WORD OF GOD?
ALL RIGHT! YOU'RE THE NEW FRESH-MEN, RIGHT?
BOING
...IT ALMOST FEELS LIKE WE'VE LUCKED OUT IN A GIRL'S SCHOOL!
WHOA!
THAT'S REALLY A GUY, RIGHT?
I'M UP-STAIRS IN 210!
COME UP ANY TIME!
HE'S HERE, SO I HOPE SO.
BUT IF YOU TAKE THOSE TWO...
...AND LINE THEM UP...

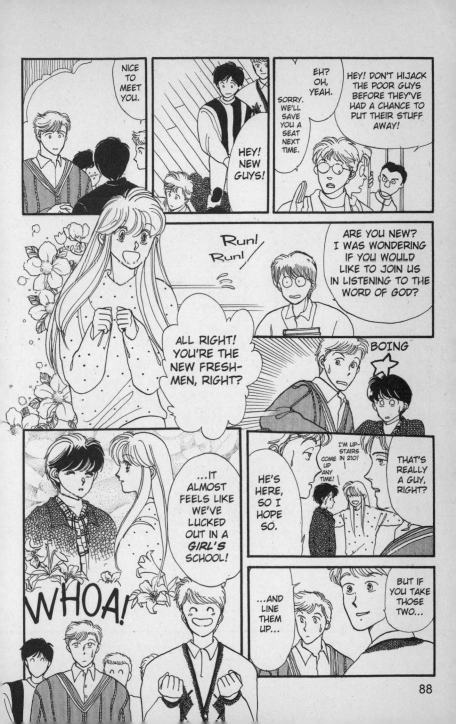

Aww, that's just stupid!
What good does it do if they only look like girls!
I'VE GOT AN ODD ONE FOR A ROOM-MATE.
BUT STILL...
I'M GLAD EVERY-BODY SEEMS NICE.
FOR A LONG TIME, I WAS WORRIED ABOUT WHO I'D END UP ROOMING WITH.
I'M GLAD IT'S YOU.
IT'S OKAY. HIS PER-SONALITY ISN'T BAD.
I'M GLAD I CAN RELY ON A BRAVE PERSON.
HEY, A GUY SHOULD RELY ON HIMSELF!
AH! YEAH, YOU'RE RIGHT.
AN ATTITUDE LIKE THAT WILL ONLY ATTRACT THE PERVERTS.
OKAY...
And with their last faint anxieties put to rest, the two began their dorm life.

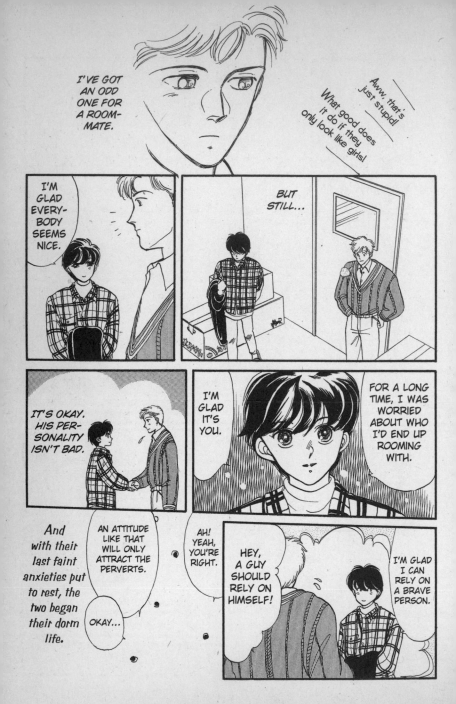

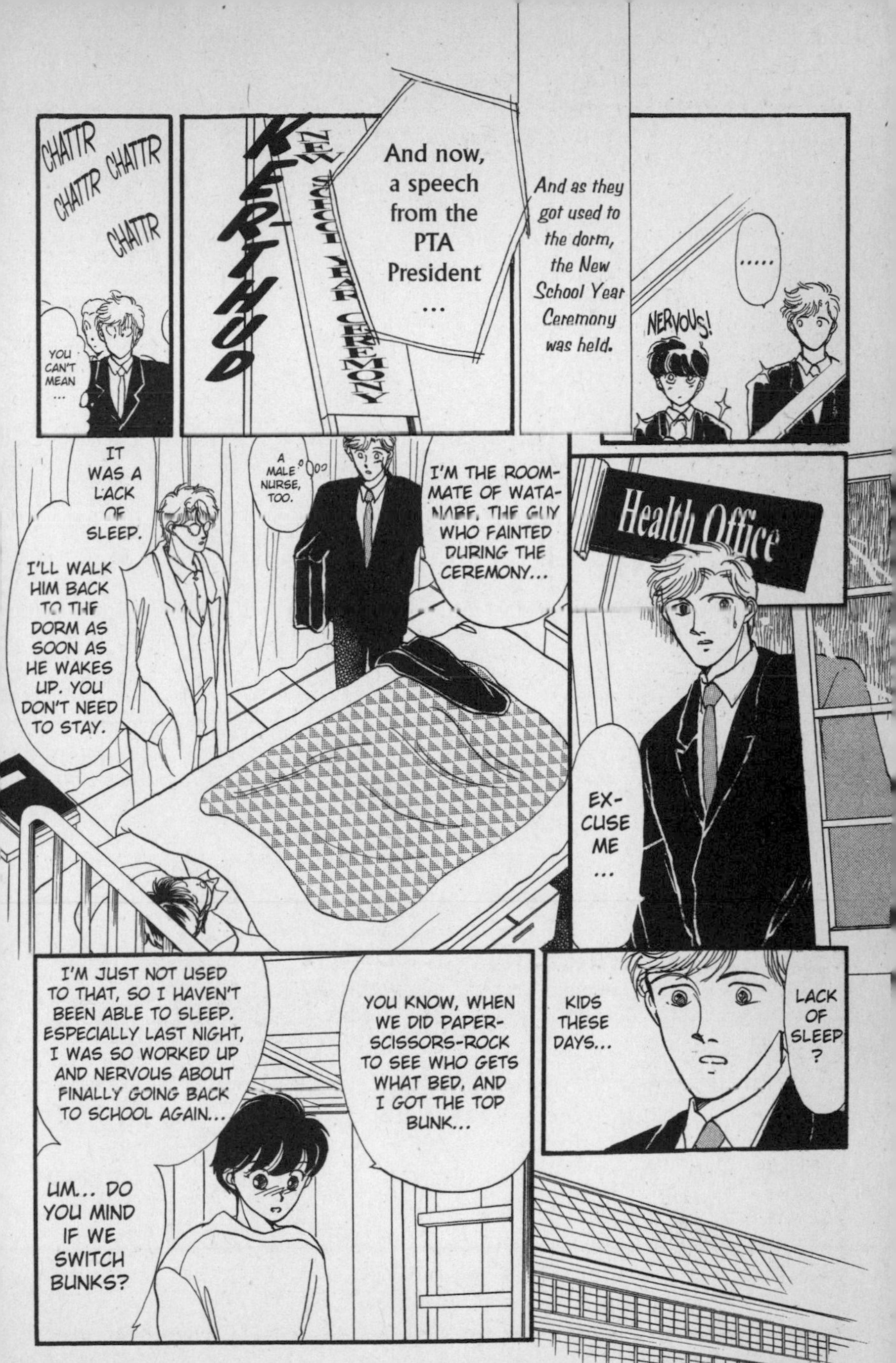

And as they got used to the dorm, the New School Year Ceremony was held.
.....
NERVOUS!
And now, a speech from the PTA President ...
NEW SCHOOL YEAR CEREMONY
KERTHUD
CHATTR CHATTR CHATTR CHATTR
YOU CAN'T MEAN ...
Health Office
EXCUSE ME ...
I'M THE ROOMMATE OF WATANABE, THE GUY WHO FAINTED DURING THE CEREMONY...
A MALE NURSE, TOO.
IT WAS A LACK OF SLEEP.
I'LL WALK HIM BACK TO THE DORM AS SOON AS HE WAKES UP. YOU DON'T NEED TO STAY.
LACK OF SLEEP?
KIDS THESE DAYS...
YOU KNOW, WHEN WE DID PAPER-SCISSORS-ROCK TO SEE WHO GETS WHAT BED, AND I GOT THE TOP BUNK...
I'M JUST NOT USED TO THAT, SO I HAVEN'T BEEN ABLE TO SLEEP. ESPECIALLY LAST NIGHT, I WAS SO WORKED UP AND NERVOUS ABOUT FINALLY GOING BACK TO SCHOOL AGAIN...
UM... DO YOU MIND IF WE SWITCH BUNKS?

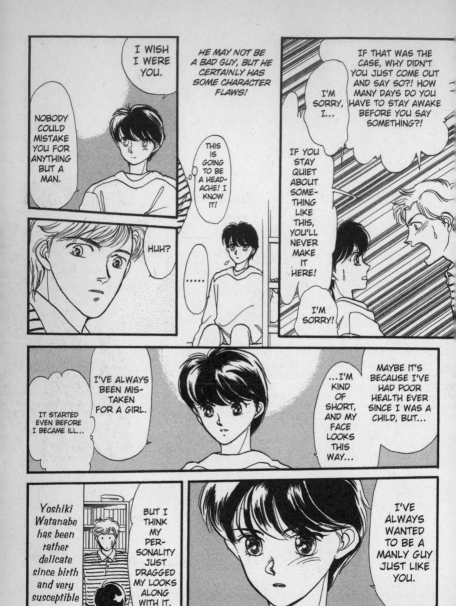

I WISH I WERE YOU.
NOBODY COULD MISTAKE YOU FOR ANYTHING BUT A MAN.
HE MAY NOT BE A BAD GUY, BUT HE CERTAINLY HAS SOME CHARACTER FLAWS!
HUH?
THIS IS GOING TO BE A HEAD-ACHE! I KNOW IT!
......
IF THAT WAS THE CASE, WHY DIDN'T YOU JUST COME OUT AND SAY SO?! HOW MANY DAYS DO YOU HAVE TO STAY AWAKE BEFORE YOU SAY SOMETHING?!
I'M SORRY, I...
IF YOU STAY QUIET ABOUT SOME-THING LIKE THIS, YOU'LL NEVER MAKE IT HERE!
I'M SORRY!
I'VE ALWAYS BEEN MIS-TAKEN FOR A GIRL.
IT STARTED EVEN BEFORE I BECAME ILL...
...I'M KIND OF SHORT, AND MY FACE LOOKS THIS WAY...
MAYBE IT'S BECAUSE I'VE HAD POOR HEALTH EVER SINCE I WAS A CHILD, BUT...
Yoshiki Watanabe has been rather delicate since birth and very susceptible to suggestion.
BUT I THINK MY PER-SONALITY JUST DRAGGED MY LOOKS ALONG WITH IT.
I'VE ALWAYS WANTED TO BE A MANLY GUY JUST LIKE YOU.

MAYBE, BUT COMPARED TO THAT GUY...
Not a care in the world!!
KISARAGI IS DIFFERENT FROM ME. HE'S COMPLETELY ACCEPTED WHO HE IS.
I'M NO-WHERE NEAR THAT.
HE WAS AWARE OF IT. SORRY FOR RUBBING IT IN.
WELL, YOU'RE ONLY 15.
IT ALL STARTS HERE.
YOU'LL GROW.
YOU REALLY THINK SO?
YOU'LL BE FINE!
IT'S KIND OF A NICE SITUA-TION.
WE'RE HERE SHARING THE SAME ROOM. I SHOULD DO WHAT I CAN TO HELP HIM.

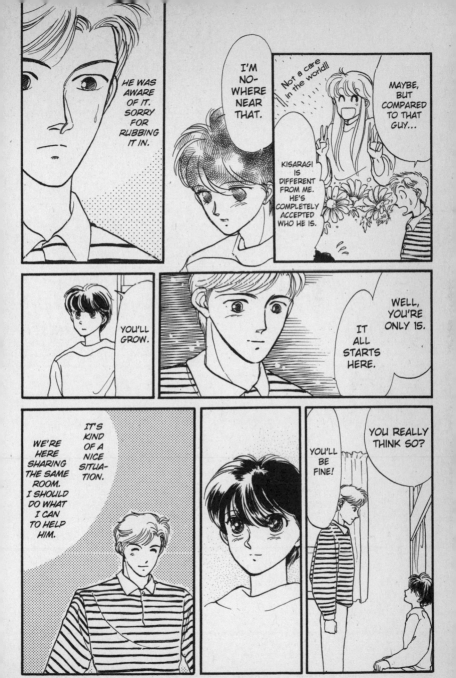

At that time...
...neither of them realized that the atmosphere of their relationship had shifted from the norm.
And time passed without incident...
...until eventually...
WHERE'S THE SCIENCE LECTURE HALL AGAIN?
THIRD FLOOR, ISN'T IT?
A wave of "self awareness" washed over.
One!! Two!! Three! And...
YAWN
OH! IT'S WATA-NABE!
B-BMP
.....
??
B-BMP

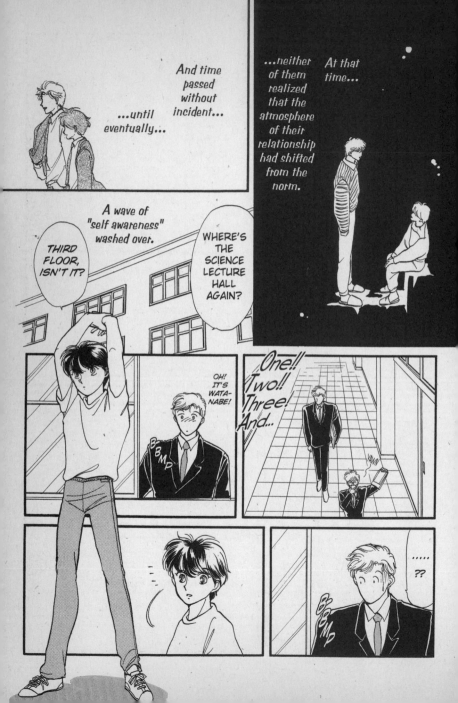

FUJIKAKE!!
FWA
THE SOUND OF A HEART LEAPING.
?
WH-WHY DO I HAVE TO HIDE?!
WHAT'S WRONG, FUJI-KAKE?
B-BMP B-BMP B-BMP
IS...
B-BMP
IS THIS...?
B-BMP
B-BMP
WHAT WAS GOING ON THIS AFTER-NOON?
117
N-NOTHING, REALLY!
IT CAN'T BE! IT CAN'T BE! IT'S IMPOSSIBLE!
I WAS SURPRISED THAT YOU SUDDENLY VANISHED.
KNOCK KNOCK
YES?

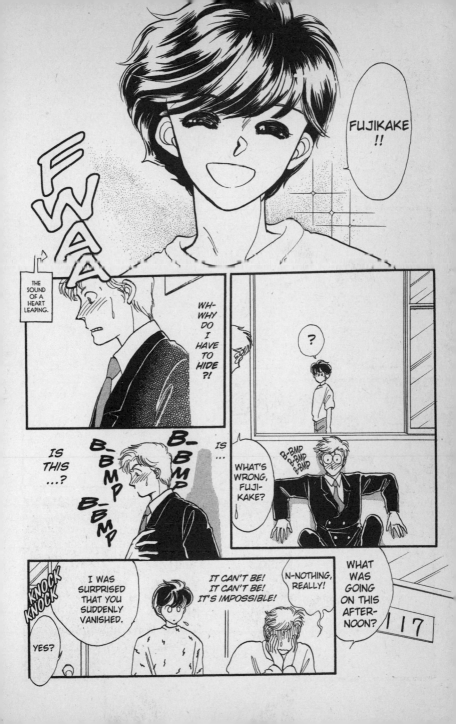

CHAKL
TP
CHAKL
CHAKL
CHAKL
CHAKL
IT CAN'T BE THAT I'M...
NO, IT CAN'T BE TRUE!
I DON'T KNOW THE RULES.
WE'LL TEACH YOU THE RULES, COME ON!
WHAT'S WRONG WITH YOU?
CHAKL
CHAKL
AM I IN LOVE WITH WATANABE?
YOSHIKI'S A MAN!
A MAN!!
GET A HOLD OF YOURSELF!
JUST CALM DOWN, TATSURO!
WHOA!
FUJIKAKE?
TWNGE
...AREN'T I?
HOMO
THEN IT MEANS...
...THAT I'M THAT NOTORIOUS WORD...

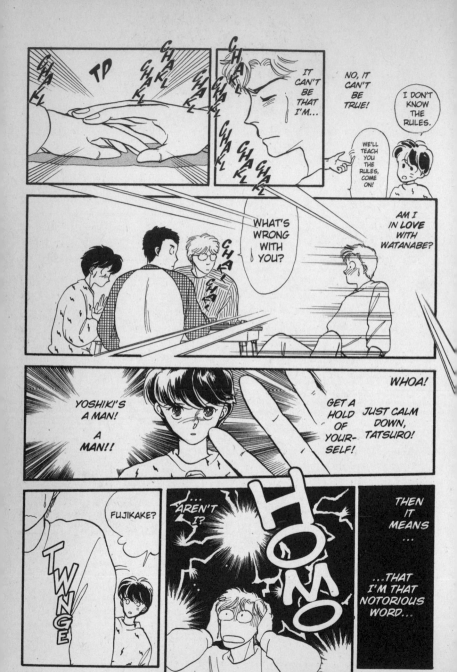

TMP TMP TMP
.....
IS SOME-THING ...
...IN PARTICULAR WORRYING YOU?
HUH?
AT A TIME LIKE THIS, YOU MUST COME TO US!
NO...
CLUSTER
UM ...
CLUSTER
NEVER FEAR! WE *CERTAINLY* AREN'T EXPECTING YOU TO TITHE AT OUR CHURCH IMMEDIATELY!
CLUSTER
I...
NOW, COME WITH US...
CLUSTER
CLUSTER
SHLUMP
AWWWWW
IT'S TIMES LIKE *THAT* WHEN YOU HAVE TO GIVE THEM A FLAT "NO"!
HUFF HUFF HUFF
I-I'M SORRY!
THAT WAS SCARY!
THANK YOU.

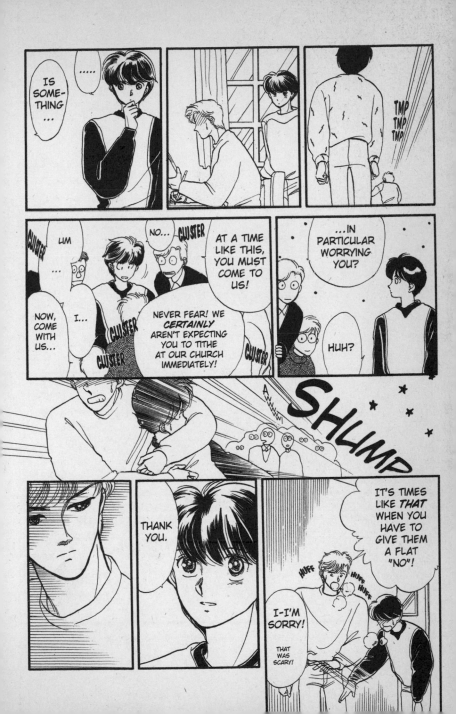

THAT SMILE LIKE THE SUN JUST CAME OUT ON A CLOUDY DAY!
AWW.
IT'S LIKE A DREAM.
OH, MAN!
THIS WAS THE LAST THING I EXPECTED TO STUMBLE UPON IN MY DORM LIFE.
I ADMIT THAT WATANABE IS CUTE.
AND I DID HAVE THE DESIRE TO PROTECT HIM.
AND I THOUGHT A BUNCH OF OTHER THINGS I DON'T WANT TO ADMIT.
BUT...
BUT...

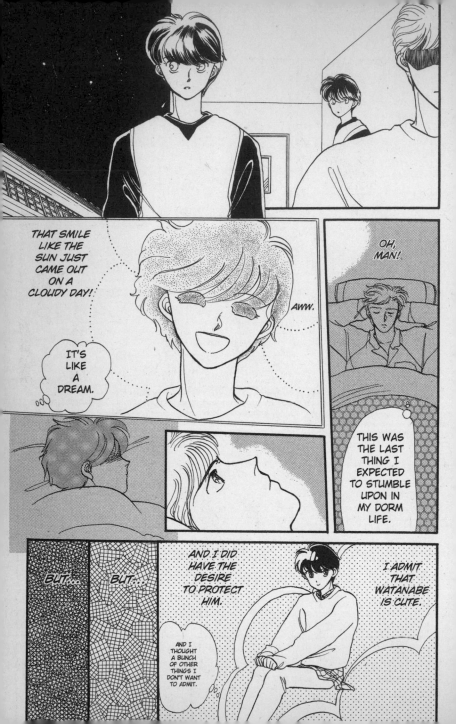

BUT HE'S A MAN!!!
I CAN'T SAY ANY MORE THAN THIS! IF I SAY IT, I WON'T BE ABLE TO TAKE IT BACK!
FATHER, MOTHER, YOUR SON WILL GIVE YOU GRAND-CHILDREN!
Tatsurō Fujikake left for Tokyo with the promise still on his lips to give them grandchildren who will inherit the mikan groves.
FUJI-KAKE?
YES...
EVEN WHEN WE'RE TOGETHER IN THE ROOM, I CAN'T TALK TO HIM...
I GET THE FEELING THAT HE'S AVOIDING ME.
HMM. WITH TWO GUYS WHO DON'T KNOW EACH OTHER SHARING THE SAME ROOM, I THINK STUFF LIKE THAT ARE BOUND TO HAPPEN.
I DON'T HAVE A ROOMMATE YET MYSELF, SO I CAN'T REALLY SAY ANYTHING.
IF THINGS GET TOO ROUGH, YOU CAN ALWAYS COME STAY WITH ME.
DON'T WORRY SO MUCH.
YES. I SHOULDN'T WORRY SO MUCH.
HUH? WASN'T THAT FUJIKAKE JUST NOW?
EH?
IT LOOKS LIKE HE WENT INTO THE ROOM NEXT TO MINE.

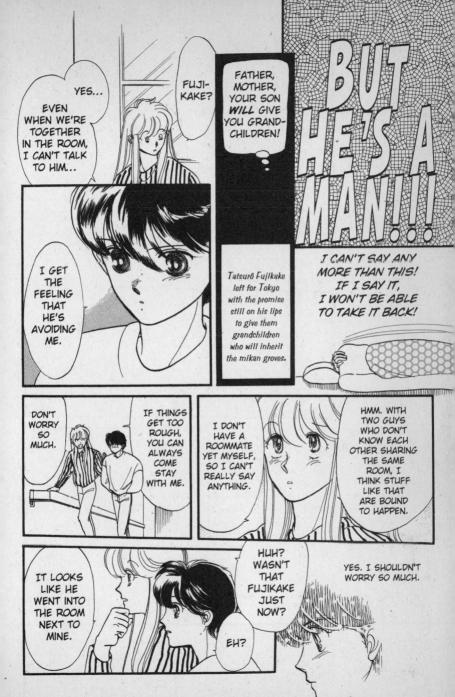

KACHAK
YOU HAVE A QUESTION FOR ME AS HEAD RESIDENT?
YOU WANT TO CHANGE ROOMS?
HMM... I WAS TOLD THAT REQUESTS LIKE THIS WOULD START COMING IN ABOUT THIS TIME OF YEAR...
BUT IT ISN'T THAT EASY TO PULL OFF. YOU'LL HAVE TO FIND SOME OTHER GUY TO SWITCH WITH.
I UNDERSTAND THAT.
DID SOMETHING HAPPEN WITH YOU AND WATANABE?
I DIDN'T DO ANYTHING TO HIM!!

BANZAI

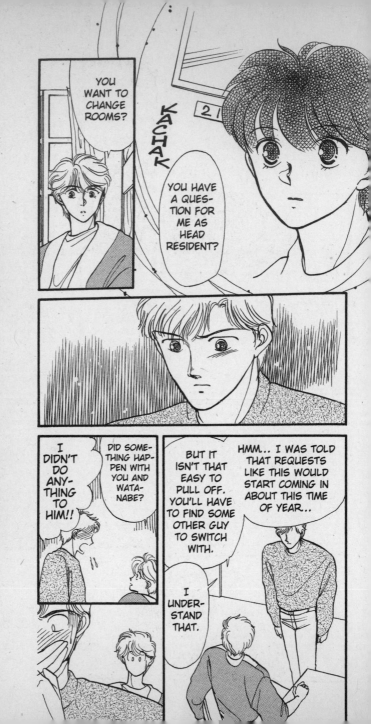

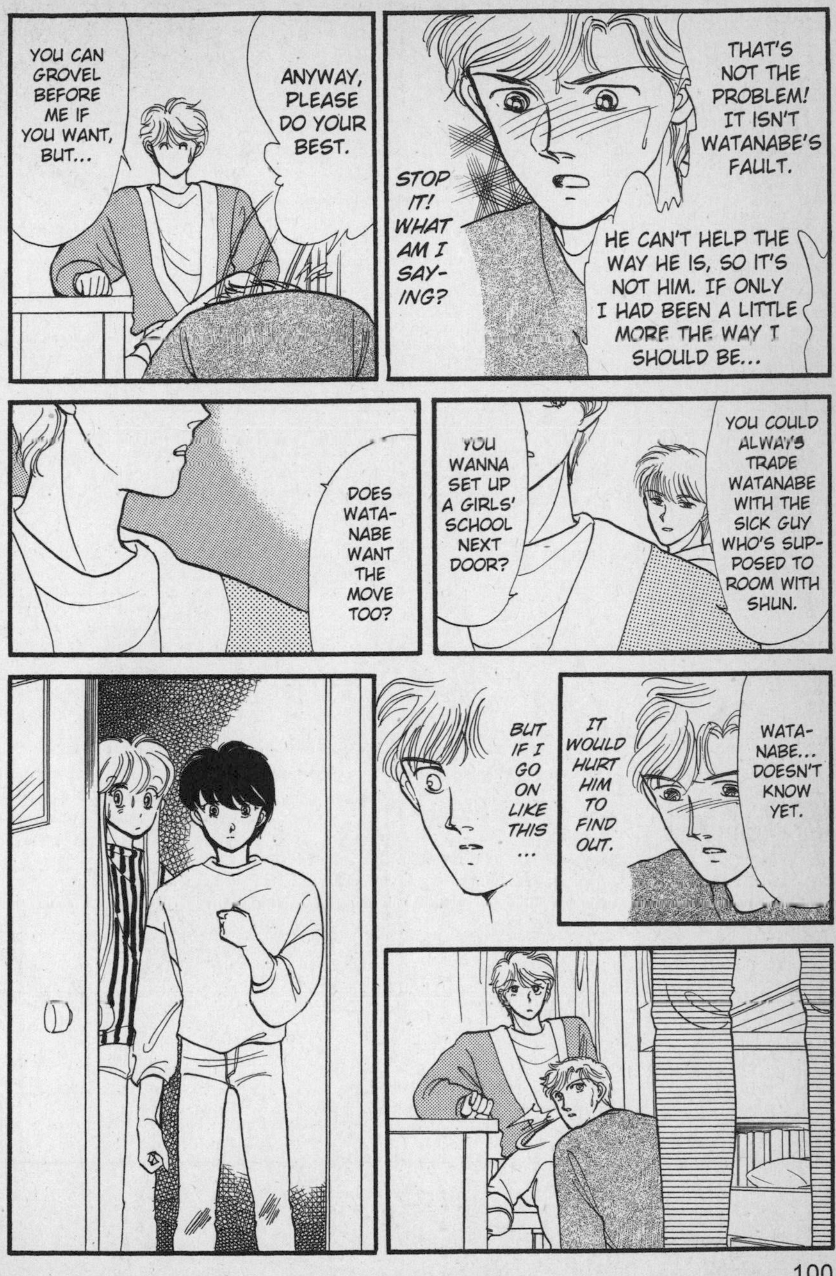
THAT'S NOT THE PROBLEM! IT ISN'T WATANABE'S FAULT.
HE CAN'T HELP THE WAY HE IS, SO IT'S NOT HIM. IF ONLY I HAD BEEN A LITTLE MORE THE WAY I SHOULD BE...
STOP IT! WHAT AM I SAYING?
ANYWAY, PLEASE DO YOUR BEST.
YOU CAN GROVEL BEFORE ME IF YOU WANT, BUT...
YOU COULD ALWAYS TRADE WATANABE WITH THE SICK GUY WHO'S SUPPOSED TO ROOM WITH SHUN.
YOU WANNA SET UP A GIRLS' SCHOOL NEXT DOOR?
DOES WATANABE WANT THE MOVE TOO?
WATANABE... DOESN'T KNOW YET.
IT WOULD HURT HIM TO FIND OUT.
BUT IF I GO ON LIKE THIS...

WATA-
NABE!!
WA--
WHAT WAS THAT?
WATANABE, WAIT!!
WATANABE ...
BAMM
KACHA

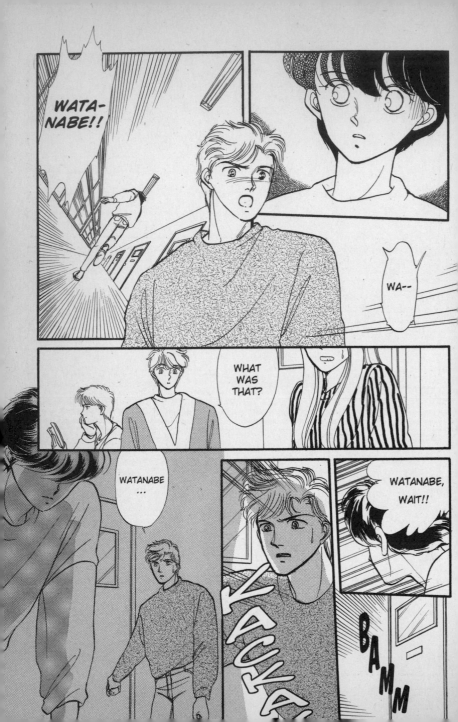

AH-HA! I'M SORRY. DID THAT SUR-PRISE YOU?
EVEN I'M NOT REALLY SURE WHY I RAN.
I'M SORRY! I DIDN'T REALIZE ...
I NEVER REALIZED THAT I WAS CAUSING YOU SO MANY PROBLEMS, FUJIKAKE...
I'M SO WISHY-WASHY THAT--
N--
NO! YOU'RE WRONG, WATANABE!
IT'S NOT...
BUT FROM NOW ON, I'LL DO MY BEST!
I'LL DO MY BEST TO NOT CAUSE PROBLEMS FOR YOU...
...SO YOU DON'T HAVE TO MOVE OUT!
IF YOU CHANGE ROOMS, I'LL JUST BE GET-TING IN SOME-BODY ELSE'S WAY.
I DON'T HAVE THE CONFIDENCE TO ROOM WITH ANYBODY ELSE BUT YOU.
BY SAYING THIS, I GUESS I'M LEANING ON YOU AGAIN...
BUT...
BUT I'M REALLY *GLAD* THAT WE'RE SHARING A ROOM.

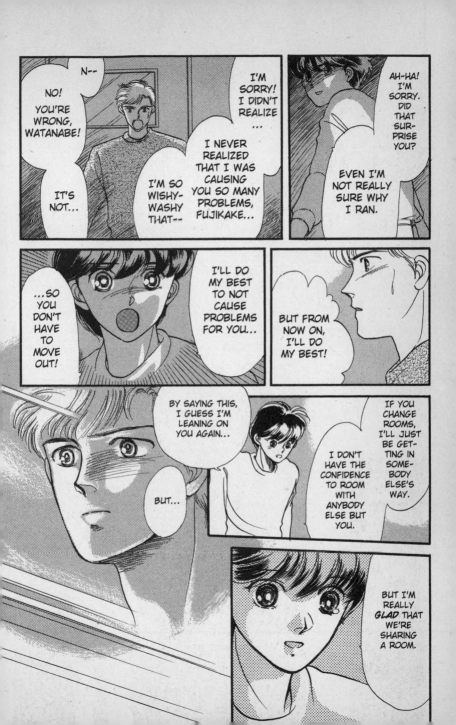

F--
F-F-F-F-
F-F-F-F-
F-F-F-F-
FUJIKAKE?
FOOL!
WHAT ARE YOU DOING, TATSURO?! HE'S A MAN!!
N-NO, YOU'RE WRONG.
CALM YOURSELF! THERE'S STILL TIME TO SAVE THE SITUATION!
BECAUSE I...
I'LL NEVER HAVE GRANDCHILDREN WITH A MAN!
I...
I LOVE YOU.
And when that happened ...

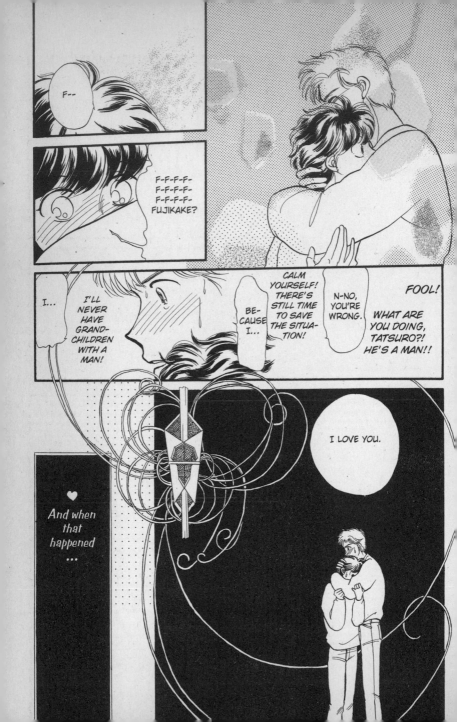

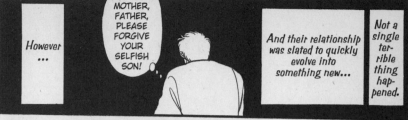

Not a single terrible thing happened.
And their relationship was slated to quickly evolve into something new...
MOTHER, FATHER, PLEASE FORGIVE YOUR SELFISH SON!
However ...
THE WAY IT IS NOW, MY FEELINGS ARE PRETTY WELL FIXED.
I LOVE FUJIKAKE, AND HE SAID THE SAME TO ME.
IT'S UNFORTUNATE FOR ME THAT I WAS BORN A MAN, BUT THERE'S NOT MUCH WE CAN DO ABOUT IT.
AND SO, THE THING I WANTED TO ASK YOU ABOUT, HASUKAWA, IS...
NEITHER OF US IS SURE HOW WE'RE SUPPOSED TO GO ABOUT THIS...
THE MR. HASUKAWA IN THE HEALTH OFFICE IS YOUR OLDER BROTHER, ISN'T HE?
I'M TOO EMBARRASSED TO GO AND ASK HIM.
DON'T YOU KNOW ABOUT THESE THINGS, HASUKAWA?
HASUKAWA?
And the sea of ignorance washed ashore and kissed the feet of young people everywhere.
AH! HE'S OUT COLD.
HOW WOULD SUKA-CHAN KNOW ABOUT STUFF LIKE THAT?
AAAH!
SHUN!
YOU WERE LISTENING?!
BOY MEETS BOY: THE END

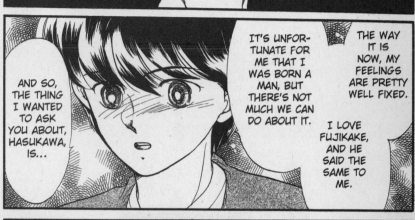

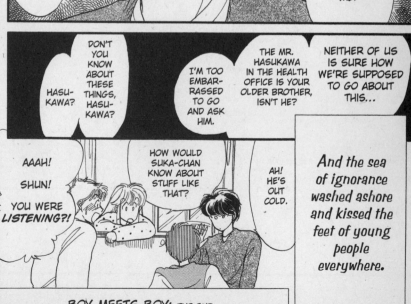

THE
JAPANESE
SUMMER
IS HERE

I'M SENDING YOU MY SYMPATHIES REGARDING THE CONTINUING HEAT.
AH...
YAWN...
THE LETHARGY OF SUMMER HAS COME UPON EVEN THE USUALLY ACTIVE RYOKURIN-RYO.
FOR THE SECOND TIME.
SHUMPHH

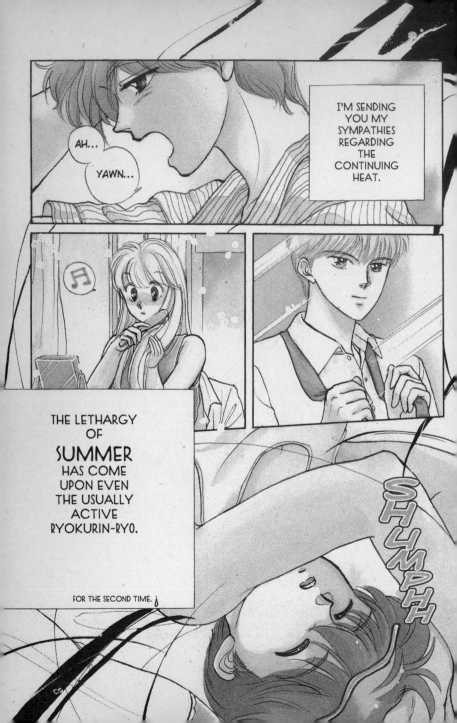

SUKA
GREEN-WOOD

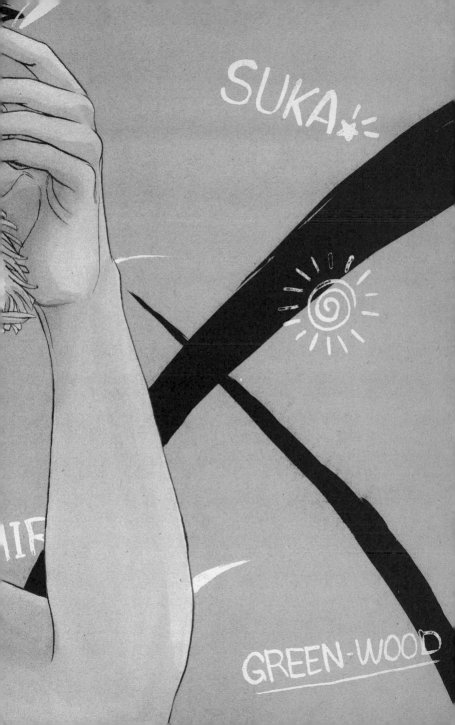

THE JAPANESE SUMMER IS HERE

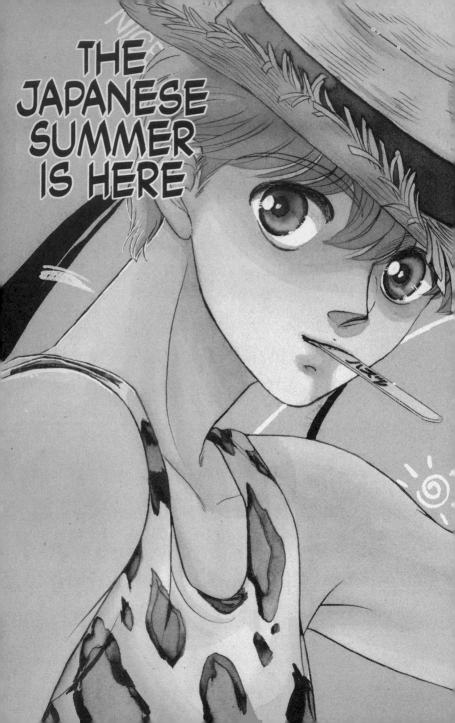

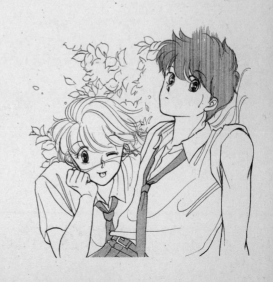

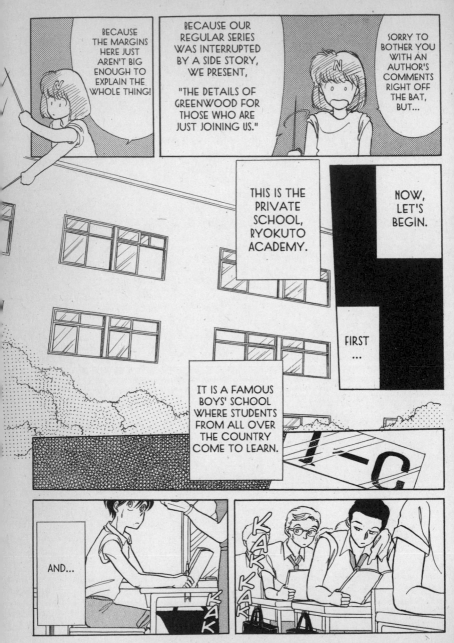

SORRY TO BOTHER YOU WITH AN AUTHOR'S COMMENTS RIGHT OFF THE BAT, BUT...
BECAUSE OUR REGULAR SERIES WAS INTERRUPTED BY A SIDE STORY, WE PRESENT,
"THE DETAILS OF GREENWOOD FOR THOSE WHO ARE JUST JOINING US."
BECAUSE THE MARGINS HERE JUST AREN'T BIG ENOUGH TO EXPLAIN THE WHOLE THING!
NOW, LET'S BEGIN.
FIRST ...
THIS IS THE PRIVATE SCHOOL, RYOKUTO ACADEMY.
IT IS A FAMOUS BOYS' SCHOOL WHERE STUDENTS FROM ALL OVER THE COUNTRY COME TO LEARN.
KAKAKAKAK
AND...
KAK KAK

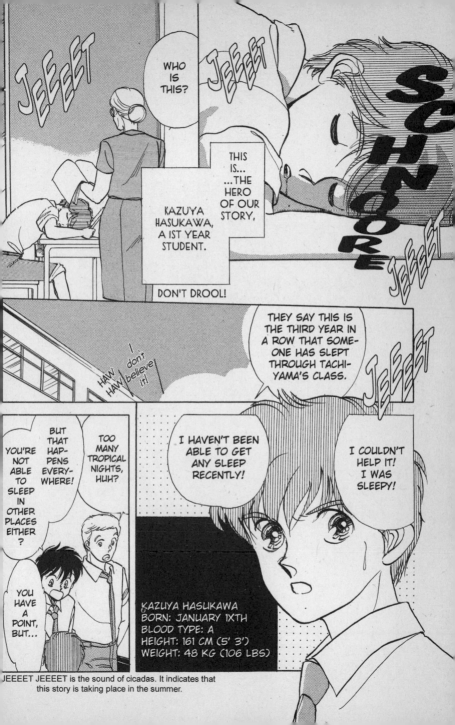

SCHNORE
JEEEET
WHO IS THIS?
JEEEET
THIS IS... ...THE HERO OF OUR STORY,
KAZUYA HASUKAWA, A 1ST YEAR STUDENT.
DON'T DROOL!
JEEEET
THEY SAY THIS IS THE THIRD YEAR IN A ROW THAT SOMEONE HAS SLEPT THROUGH TACHIYAMA'S CLASS.
I don't believe it!
HAW HAW
I COULDN'T HELP IT! I WAS SLEEPY!
I HAVEN'T BEEN ABLE TO GET ANY SLEEP RECENTLY!
KAZUYA HASUKAWA
BORN: JANUARY 1XTH
BLOOD TYPE: A
HEIGHT: 161 CM (5' 3')
WEIGHT: 48 KG (106 LBS)
TOO MANY TROPICAL NIGHTS, HUH?
BUT THAT HAPPENS EVERYWHERE!
YOU'RE NOT ABLE TO SLEEP IN OTHER PLACES EITHER?
YOU HAVE A POINT, BUT...

JEEEET JEEEET is the sound of cicadas. It indicates that this story is taking place in the summer.

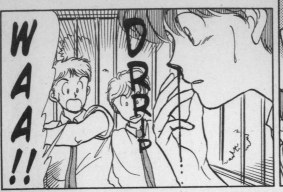

STILL PLAYING THE INVALID!
WHAP
DRRIP
WAAA!!
.....
WOW, IT'S BEEN A LONG TIME SINCE THAT HAPPENED, HUH?
I DIDN'T HIT YOU THAT HARD ...
RUSTL RUSTL
HASU-KAWA ...
WHEN THINGS LIKE THAT HAPPEN ...
PAPP
THE HEALTH OFFICE! HE SHOULD GO TO THE HEALTH OFFICE!
WHA --?
OH! YOU'RE RIGHT! LET'S TAKE HIM THERE!
H-HOLD IT! I'M NOT GOING TO ANY HEALTH OFFICE...
WHAT ARE YOU SAYING? YOUR NOSE-BLEED IS SO BAD, YOU'RE ABOUT TO DIE!
LET GO!
GRMP
YOU GUYS JUST WANT TO TAKE ME THERE BECAUSE THE OFFICE IS AIR-CONDITIONED!
EXACTLY. HIS BRAIN'S STILL INTACT!
THANK GOODNESS! I WAS WORRIED ABOUT THAT!

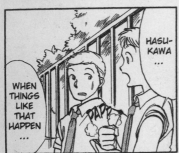

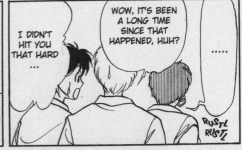

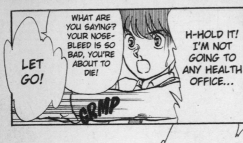

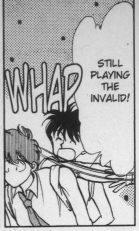

THE "NURSE" IN THIS BOYS' SCHOOL IS A MAN.
Health Office
EVER SINCE YOU WERE A KID ...
SQEEZ
... WHEN YOU WERE FATIGUED OR LACKED SLEEP, YOUR BODY WOULD REACT WITH A NOSEBLEED.
ESPECIALLY DURING THE SUMMER WHEN IT'S HARDER TO SLEEP.
AND AT TIMES LIKE THAT I...
...WOULD TRY TO HELP YOU SLEEP...
...BY PLACING A DAMP TOWEL ON YOUR FORE-HEAD AND CALLING IN OTHER FAMILY MEMBERS TO WATCH OVER YOU.
AND NOW YOU LOOK AT THIS KIND BROTHER OF YOURS...
KAZUHIRO HASUKAWA. KAZUYA'S OLDER BROTHER (MARRIED).
...AND GIVE ME ATTITUDE!
Ah, it's so cool!
It's paradise! Paradise!

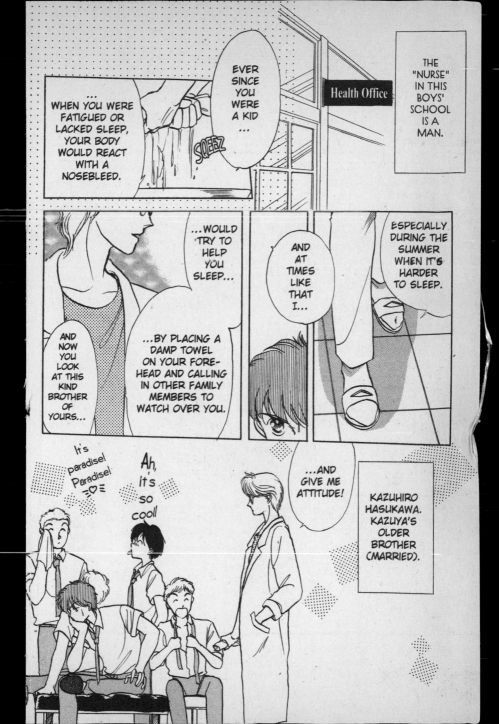

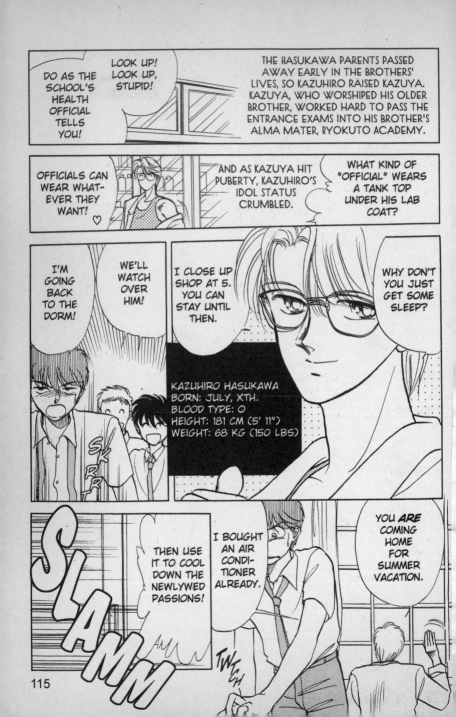

THE HASUKAWA PARENTS PASSED AWAY EARLY IN THE BROTHERS' LIVES, SO KAZUHIRO RAISED KAZUYA. KAZUYA, WHO WORSHIPED HIS OLDER BROTHER, WORKED HARD TO PASS THE ENTRANCE EXAMS INTO HIS BROTHER'S ALMA MATER, RYOKUTO ACADEMY.
LOOK UP! LOOK UP, STUPID!
DO AS THE SCHOOL'S HEALTH OFFICIAL TELLS YOU!
WHAT KIND OF "OFFICIAL" WEARS A TANK TOP UNDER HIS LAB COAT?
AND AS KAZUYA HIT PUBERTY, KAZUHIRO'S IDOL STATUS CRUMBLED.
OFFICIALS CAN WEAR WHAT-EVER THEY WANT! ♡
WHY DON'T YOU JUST GET SOME SLEEP?
I CLOSE UP SHOP AT 5. YOU CAN STAY UNTIL THEN.
KAZUHIRO HASUKAWA
BORN: JULY, XTH.
BLOOD TYPE: O
HEIGHT: 181 CM (5' 11")
WEIGHT: 68 KG (150 LBS)
WE'LL WATCH OVER HIM!
I'M GOING BACK TO THE DORM!
SKRRT
YOU ARE COMING HOME FOR SUMMER VACATION.
I BOUGHT AN AIR CONDI-TIONER ALREADY.
THEN USE IT TO COOL DOWN THE NEWLYWED PASSIONS!
TWITCH
SLAMM

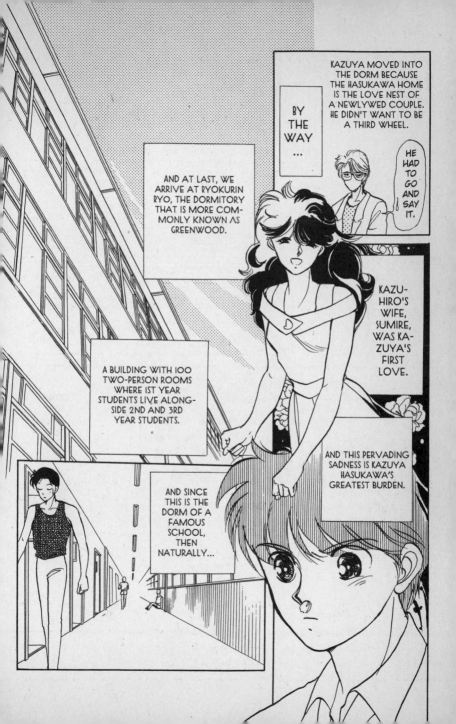

BY THE WAY ...
KAZUYA MOVED INTO THE DORM BECAUSE THE HASUKAWA HOME IS THE LOVE NEST OF A NEWLYWED COUPLE. HE DIDN'T WANT TO BE A THIRD WHEEL.
HE HAD TO GO AND SAY IT.
KAZUHIRO'S WIFE, SUMIRE, WAS KAZUYA'S FIRST LOVE.
AND THIS PERVADING SADNESS IS KAZUYA HASUKAWA'S GREATEST BURDEN.
AND AT LAST, WE ARRIVE AT RYOKURIN RYO, THE DORMITORY THAT IS MORE COMMONLY KNOWN AS GREENWOOD.
A BUILDING WITH 100 TWO-PERSON ROOMS WHERE 1ST YEAR STUDENTS LIVE ALONGSIDE 2ND AND 3RD YEAR STUDENTS.
AND SINCE THIS IS THE DORM OF A FAMOUS SCHOOL, THEN NATURALLY...

IT IS A PLACE WHERE THE ELITE LIVE.
OR SHOULD LIVE.
PRO-BABLY.
OH, COME ON! TURN ON THE WATER IN THE BATHS!
YOU DON'T HAVE TO HEAT IT!
Office
YOUR FEES WILL GO UP.
THERE ARE ALL SORTS OF STUDENTS GATHERED HERE.
BONDA—FULLY RECOVERED!
JUST CONSIDER THIS HEAT A TEST SENT BY GOD!!
THERE ARE RELI-GIOUS GROUPS.
Bonda-sempai! Hang in there!
THERE ARE THOSE MAKING MONEY.
Refrigerator Rental Space Available
Starting at
20 yen/hour*.
Game Center Room 202.
See Aoki or Sakaguchi!
The Latest Dragon Quest is now online!!
First come, first served!!

* 15 CENTS

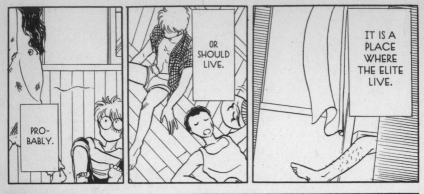

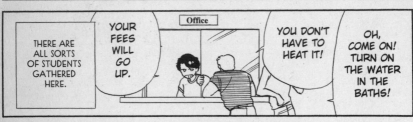

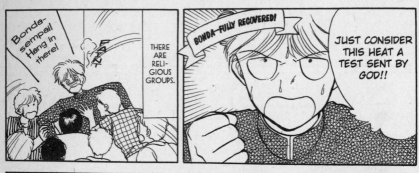

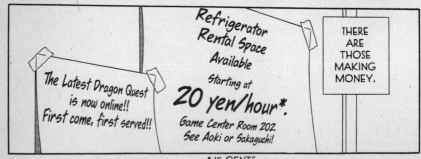

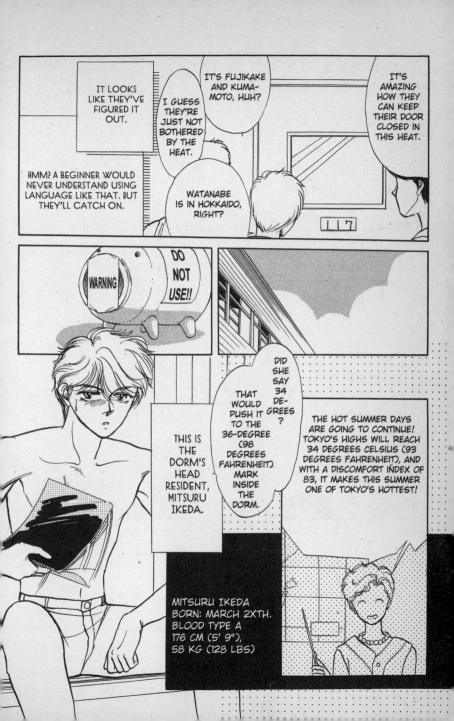

IT'S AMAZING HOW THEY CAN KEEP THEIR DOOR CLOSED IN THIS HEAT.
IT'S FUJIKAKE AND KUMA-MOTO, HUH?
I GUESS THEY'RE JUST NOT BOTHERED BY THE HEAT.
WATANABE IS IN HOKKAIDO, RIGHT?
117
IT LOOKS LIKE THEY'VE FIGURED IT OUT.
HMM? A BEGINNER WOULD NEVER UNDERSTAND USING LANGUAGE LIKE THAT. BUT THEY'LL CATCH ON.
DO NOT USE!!
WARNING
THE HOT SUMMER DAYS ARE GOING TO CONTINUE! TOKYO'S HIGHS WILL REACH 34 DEGREES CELSIUS (93 DEGREES FAHRENHEIT), AND WITH A DISCOMFORT INDEX OF 83, IT MAKES THIS SUMMER ONE OF TOKYO'S HOTTEST!
DID SHE SAY 34 DE-GREES?
THAT WOULD PUSH IT TO THE 36-DEGREE (98 DEGREES FAHRENHEIT) MARK INSIDE THE DORM.
THIS IS THE DORM'S HEAD RESIDENT, MITSURU IKEDA.
MITSURU IKEDA
BORN: MARCH 2XTH.
BLOOD TYPE A
176 CM (5' 9"),
58 KG (128 LBS)

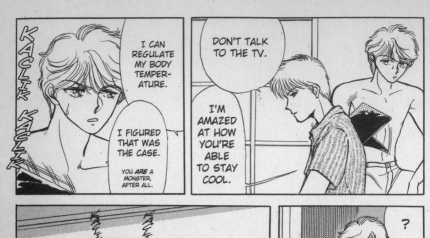

DON'T TALK TO THE TV.
I'M AMAZED AT HOW YOU'RE ABLE TO STAY COOL.
I CAN REGULATE MY BODY TEMPER-ATURE.
KACLIK KACLIK
I FIGURED THAT WAS THE CASE.
YOU ARE A MONSTER, AFTER ALL.
?
KACLIK KACLIK
KACLIK KACLIK
WHAT'S WRONG?
NOTHING.
IT'S ALL RIGHT.
TSK! HE'S HIDING!
THE PICTURES WE DID GET WILL FETCH A PRETTY HIGH PRICE. ♡
AWWWW! DAMMIT.
I DON'T FEEL LIKE DOING ANYTHING!

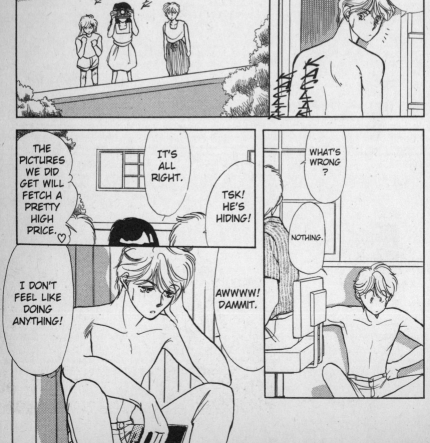

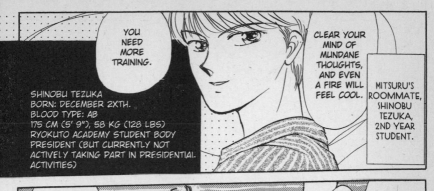

MITSURU'S ROOMMATE, SHINOBU TEZUKA, 2ND YEAR STUDENT.
CLEAR YOUR MIND OF MUNDANE THOUGHTS, AND EVEN A FIRE WILL FEEL COOL.
YOU NEED MORE TRAINING.
SHINOBU TEZUKA
BORN: DECEMBER 2XTH.
BLOOD TYPE: AB
175 CM (5' 9"), 58 KG (128 LBS)
RYOKUTO ACADEMY STUDENT BODY PRESIDENT (BUT CURRENTLY NOT ACTIVELY TAKING PART IN PRESIDENTIAL ACTIVITIES)
OH, NO ?
I WONDER ABOUT THAT. LET'S TEST IT OUT...
FLSH
MR. HEAD RESIDENT, ISN'T AN OPEN FLAME AGAINST DORM RULES?
WHERE ARE YOU GOING?
THE BATH-ROOM.
Hmmmmm...
SHMP
I'M OFF TO TOR-TURE MY NEXT-DOOR NEIGH-BOR.
THIS IS THE 2ND FLOOR, ROOM 211.
NEXT-DOOR IS ROOM 210.

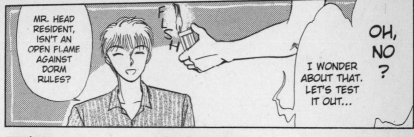

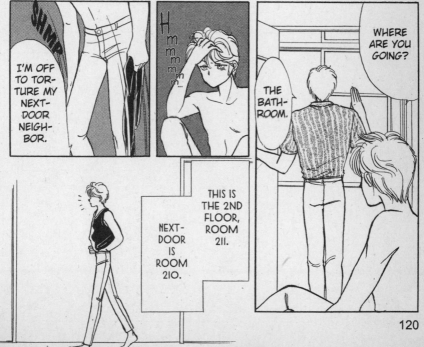

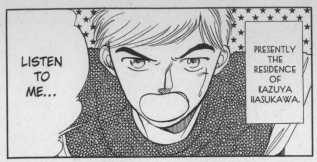

PRESENTLY THE RESIDENCE OF KAZUYA HASUKAWA.
LISTEN TO ME...
...THERE HAS NEVER BEEN A TIME WHEN IT MADE ME ANGRIER THAT YOU ARE A MAN!
HEH-HEH-HEHHHH!
YO.
OH, MIT-SURU.
You jerk! How can you look at your sempai and laugh at him?!
AAAAAAAH!
SUKA? WHAT ARE YOU UP TO?
DOING MY ASSIGNMENT.
OH! "SUKA" REFERS TO HASU-KAWA.

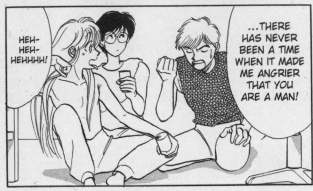

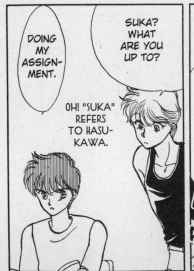

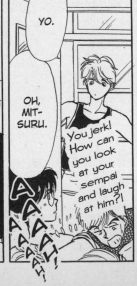

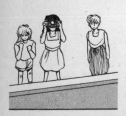

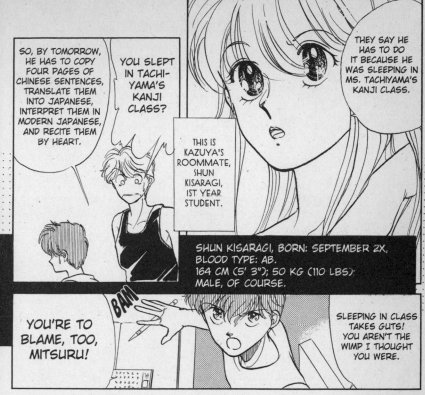

THEY SAY HE HAS TO DO IT BECAUSE HE WAS SLEEPING IN MS. TACHIYAMA'S KANJI CLASS.
YOU SLEPT IN TACHI-YAMA'S KANJI CLASS?
SO, BY TOMORROW, HE HAS TO COPY FOUR PAGES OF CHINESE SENTENCES, TRANSLATE THEM INTO JAPANESE, INTERPRET THEM IN MODERN JAPANESE, AND RECITE THEM BY HEART.
THIS IS KAZUYA'S ROOMMATE, SHUN KISARAGI, 1ST YEAR STUDENT.
SHUN KISARAGI, BORN: SEPTEMBER 2X, BLOOD TYPE: AB. 164 CM (5' 3"); 50 KG (110 LBS). MALE, OF COURSE.
SLEEPING IN CLASS TAKES GUTS! YOU AREN'T THE WIMP I THOUGHT YOU WERE.
BAM
YOU'RE TO BLAME, TOO, MITSURU!
YOU'RE ALWAYS MAKING NOISE NEXT DOOR UNTIL LATE INTO THE NIGHT AND KEEPING ME AWAKE!
IN A DORM WITH TOO LITTLE SOUND PROOFING TO BEGIN WITH, WE HAVE TO LEAVE THE DOOR OPEN IN THE HEAT...
BUT THAT APPLIES TO EVERY-BODY!
IN ANY CASE ...
I HAVE MY ASSIGNMENT. IF YOU'RE GOING TO MAKE NOISE, TAKE IT ELSEWHERE.

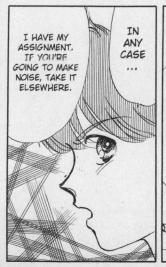

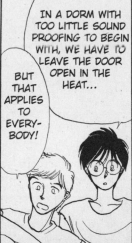

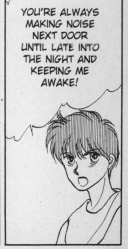

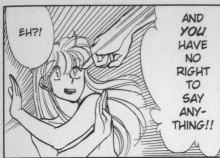

BUT SUKA-CHAN, YOU'RE OVERSENSITIVE TO ALL SORTS OF WEIRD THINGS.
IT'S SUCH A PAIN IN THE BUTT!
AND *YOU* HAVE NO RIGHT TO SAY ANY-THING!!
EH?!
IT'S HOT!
IT'S SO HOT!
AND THE MOS-QUITOES ARE KILLING ME!
I HATE THIS!
GRMBL GRMBL
GRUMBLE GRUMBLE
MUMBLE MUMBLE
GAMPH
SHUN!!
IT'S HOT...
ZZZZZZZZ
.....
WHAT DO YOU WANT?! IF I DON'T LET THE STRESS OUT, I'LL JUST FEEL HOTTER!
YOU'RE JUST COMPLAINING BECAUSE IT'S TOO HOT UNDERNEATH THAT HEAD OF THICK, LONG HAIR!!
GRR! WHAT DOES MY HAIR HAVE TO DO WITH *YOU*, SUKA-CHAN?!
Aaahh!
Ah!
IT'S TOO HOT TO GET SO ANGRY!

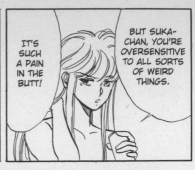

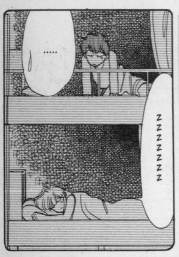

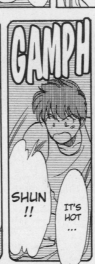

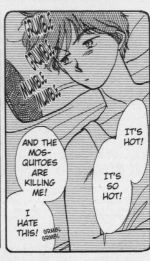

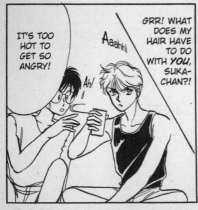

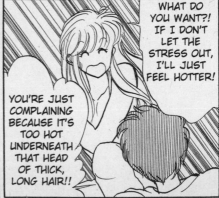

IN ANY CASE, WE CAN'T JUST SIT HERE WILTING.
RIGHT! WE HAVE TO THINK OF A WAY TO COOL OFF.
SOME-THING THAT DOESN'T REQUIRE MONEY.
HMMMMMMM..
....
WILT
AHH! I'M WORN OUT!

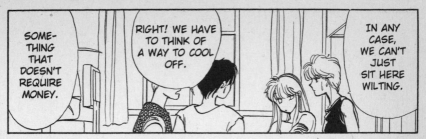

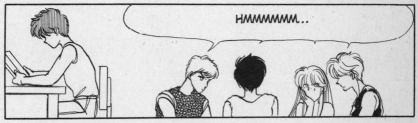

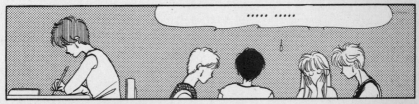

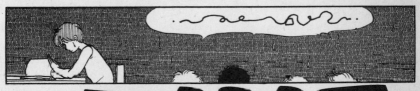

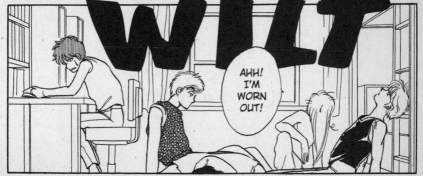

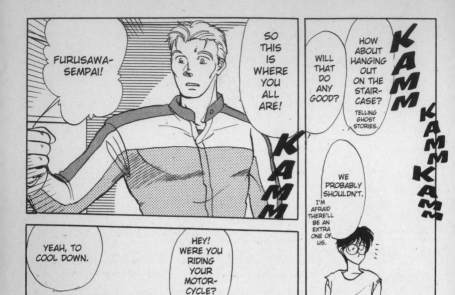

HOW ABOUT HANGING OUT ON THE STAIR-CASE? TELLING GHOST STORIES.
WILL THAT DO ANY GOOD?
KAMM KAMM KAMM KAMM
WE PROBABLY SHOULDN'T.
I'M AFRAID THERE'LL BE AN EXTRA ONE OF US.
SO THIS IS WHERE YOU ALL ARE!
KAMM
FURUSAWA-SEMPAI!
HEY! WERE YOU RIDING YOUR MOTOR-CYCLE?
YEAH, TO COOL DOWN.
THEY GAVE ME SOME EXTRA STUFF AT MY PART-TIME JOB.
HERE YOU GO.
HEY! THERE'S BEER IN HERE!
THANKS, GENERAL FURUSAWA!
MR. C.E.O. !!
YOU LOOK INCREDIBLE IN THAT LONG-SLEEVED COAT. AREN'T YOU HOT?
YEAH, I *AM* PRETTY HOT.
TH IS A BA BA MAN !

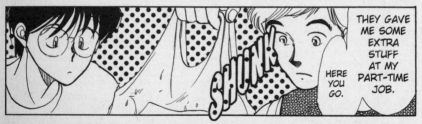

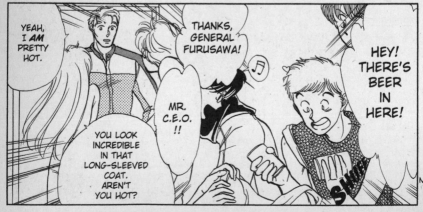

WHOOSH
I GUESS I'LL TAKE IT OFF.
WAA!!
Y-YOU REALLY ARE AMAZING!
I GUESS BIKERS ARE JUST SO TOUGH!
BUT THIS HEAT CAN REALLY AFFECT YOU.
OH, NO! NOT YOU!
NO, IT AFFECTS YOUR CONCENTRATION.
I EVEN TIPPED MY BIKE OVER ON A CORNER.
PSHUUSHH

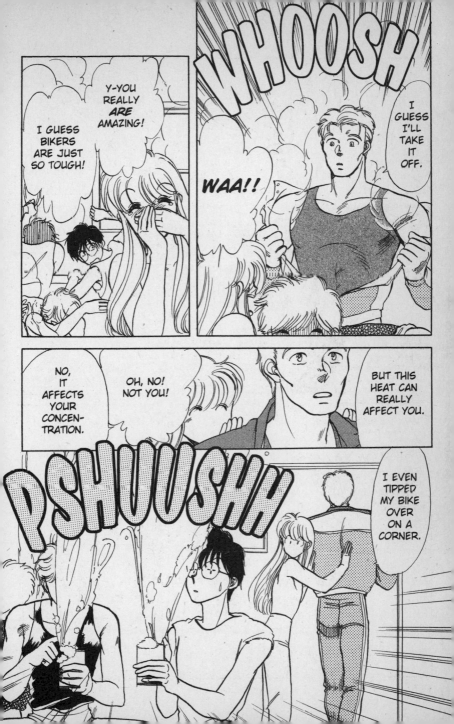

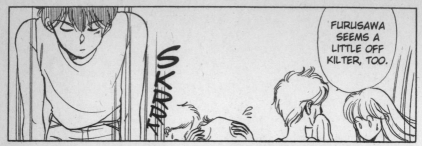

FURUSAWA SEEMS A LITTLE OFF KILTER, TOO.
WHERE ARE YOU GOING, HASU-KAWA?
I'M GOING TO LOOK FOR SOME-PLACE COOLER.
IT'S THE SAME ALL OVER THE DORM.
AIN'T NO SUCH PLACE!
THE CLOSEST GOOD SPOT IS THE LIBRARY, WHICH IS A 30-MINUTE WALK FROM HERE!
BRING YOUR COMPLAINTS TO THE WARD OFFICE.
THEN I'LL FIND SOMEPLACE *QUIETER* IN THE DORM.
WHAT'S THIS? I THOUGHT YOU LEFT YOUR ROOM, BUT YOU'RE JUST BROILING OUT HERE IN THE HALL.
OH, GIMME A BREAK!

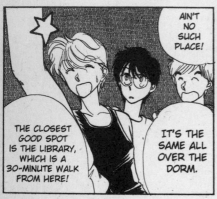

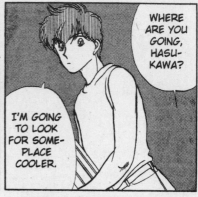

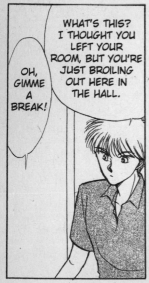

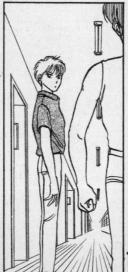

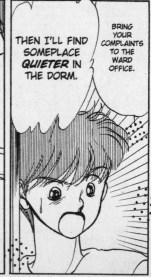

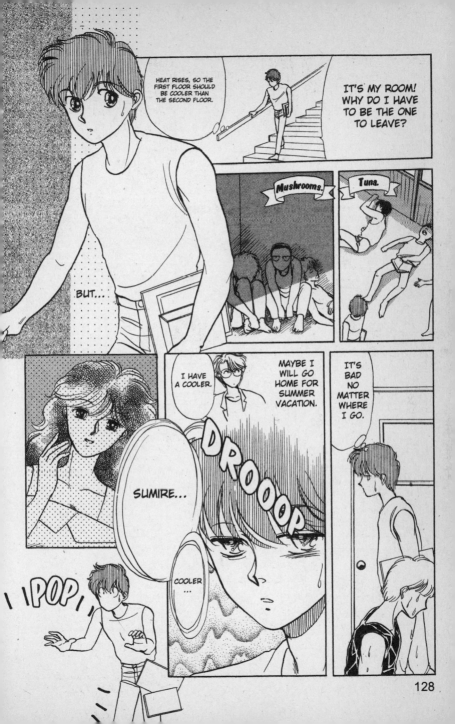

IT'S MY ROOM! WHY DO I HAVE TO BE THE ONE TO LEAVE?
HEAT RISES, SO THE FIRST FLOOR SHOULD BE COOLER THAN THE SECOND FLOOR.
BUT...
Mushrooms.
Tuna.
IT'S BAD NO MATTER WHERE I GO.
MAYBE I WILL GO HOME FOR SUMMER VACATION.
I HAVE A COOLER.
DROOOP
SUMIRE...
COOLER ...
POP

I ALREADY EXPERIENCED STAYING BEHIND LAST YEAR!
BONG
A-A MIRAGE?
WHAT AM I THINKING?
DURING SUMMER VACATION, ALMOST EVERYBODY LEAVES, SO IT WON'T FEEL AS HOT!
KATAK
A BAT?
I have a bad feeling...
STMP STMP STMP
KA-WHAK
WAAA!! WHAT ARE YOU DOING?!

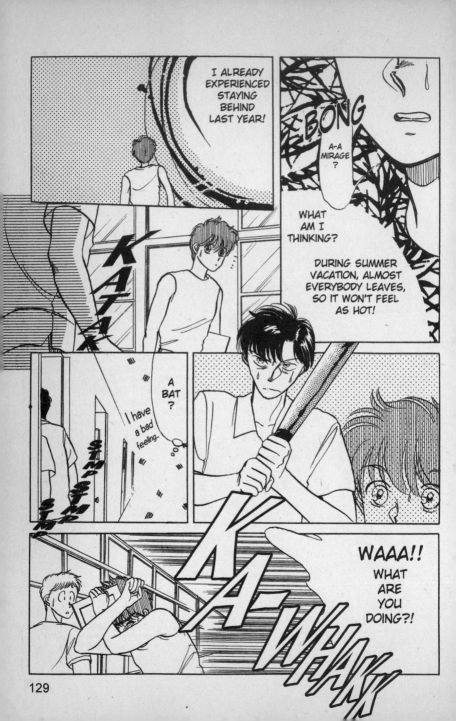

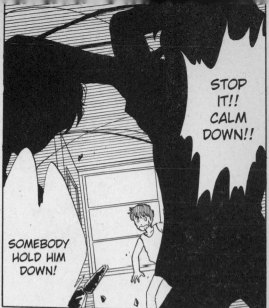

STOP IT!! CALM DOWN!!
SOMEBODY HOLD HIM DOWN!
I TOLD YOU TO STOP THAT NOISE!!
Huh? What's up?
Well, it finally happened.
CALL THE SEMPAI!
WHAT ARE YOU SO SURPRISED ABOUT?
I'VE TOLD YOU A THOUSAND TIMES!
PANT PANT
THE SONIC-WAVE ANTI-MOSQUITO DEVICE WORKS BETTER THAN THE ANTI-MOSQUITO INCENSE BURNER!
OUT TO AN EFFECTIVE RANGE OF 20 METERS!
PEEEEEEEEEEEEEEE
IT ELIMINATES THE THREAT OF FIRE IN THE DORM, AND IT EVEN HAS ANTI-MOSQUITO BENEFITS FOR YOUR ROOM!!
BUT I CAN'T STAND THAT HORRIBLE NOISE!!
W-WAIT A MINUTE.
THEN YOU MUST BE A MOSQUITO YOURSELF!!
SHUT UP!!

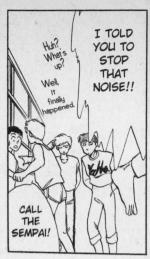

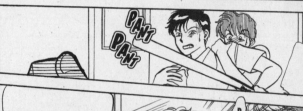

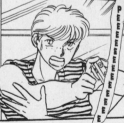

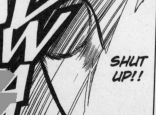

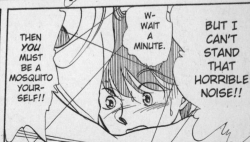

SPLAASH!!
FOR GOD'S SAKE!
CAN'T ANYBODY STAY SANE?
IT GETS A LITTLE HOT OUT, AND YOU GUYS JUST COMPLETELY GO BERSERK!!
THERE ARE QUITE A FEW PEOPLE IN THE WORLD THAT CAN HANDLE THE HEAT!
AND THERE ARE PEOPLE WHO ARE NOT JUST SUFFERING FROM THE HEAT, BUT ALSO SICK OR STARVING!
AND YOU, HEALTHY YOUNG MEN, ARE JUST HOT!
DON'T YOU THINK THIS IS PATHETIC? ARE YOU WHAT JAPAN IS COMING TO?
HASUKAWA, LET'S GO!
AND MAKE SURE THIS PLACE IS CLEANED UP!
Y-YES, SIR!
Y-YES, SIR!
HUMPH

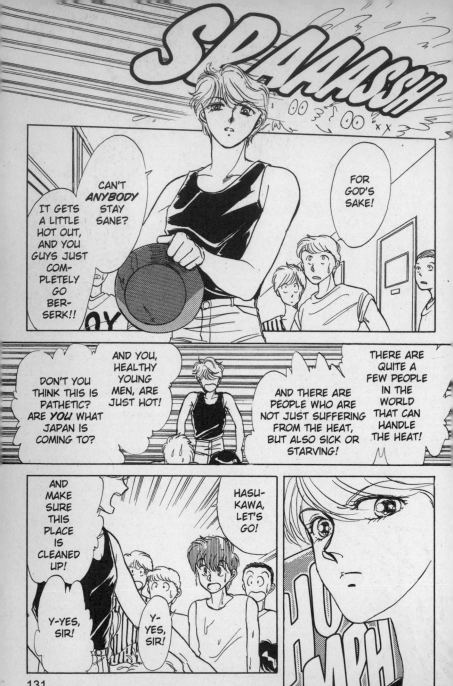

AH... THAT FELT GOOD.
.....
BUT WE'RE THE ONES WITH THE NORMAL NERVOUS SYSTEM.
I COULD CRY TEARS OF SHAME!
IT WAS JUST A COUPLE OF GUYS FREAKING OUT.
I GUESS THE ONLY ONE WHO ISN'T AFFECTED IS SHINOBU.
THE BATH-ROOM AGAIN?
TWIK
TMP TMP
WHAT'S THE MEANING OF THIS?

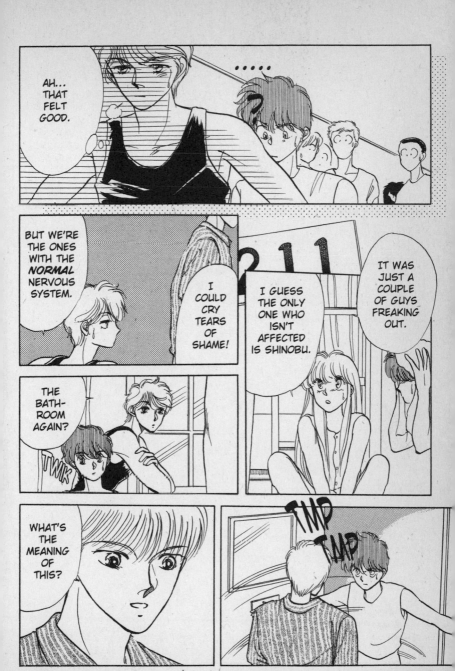

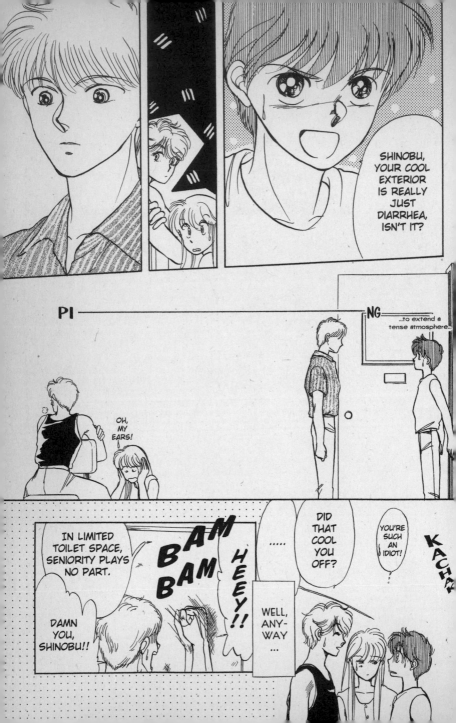

SHINOBU, YOUR COOL EXTERIOR IS REALLY JUST DIARRHEA, ISN'T IT?
PI—NG
...to extend a tense atmosphere...
OH, MY EARS!
KACHA
YOU'RE SUCH AN IDIOT!
DID THAT COOL YOU OFF?
.....
HEEEY!!
BAM BAM
IN LIMITED TOILET SPACE, SENIORITY PLAYS NO PART.
DAMN YOU, SHINOBU!!
WELL, ANY-WAY ...

I'M NOT GETTING ANYWHERE ON THIS ASSIGNMENT!
I'M OFF TO SLEEP.
THAT'S THE KIND OF PLACE GREENWOOD IS.
NOW YOU SEE, DON'T YOU? IF SO, PLEASE STAY WITH US A WHILE. ♡
NNNNN
MMBL MMBL
I'LL NEVER GET ANY SLEEP!
NNNN
NOD NOD
ZZZZZ
IT SOUNDS LIKE HE'S SUFFO-CATING.
ISN'T IT GOOD THAT HE'S SLEEPING AT ALL?
SHI-NOBU...
IT LOOKS LIKE THE HOT SEASON WILL CONTINUE ON.

THE JAPANESE SUMMER IS HERE: THE END

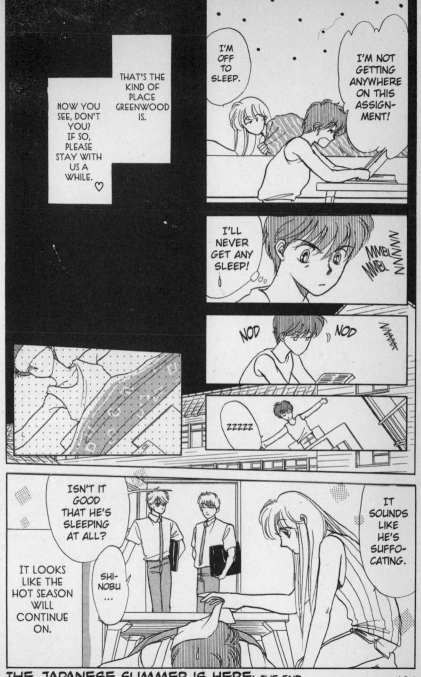

POOLSIDE MAN

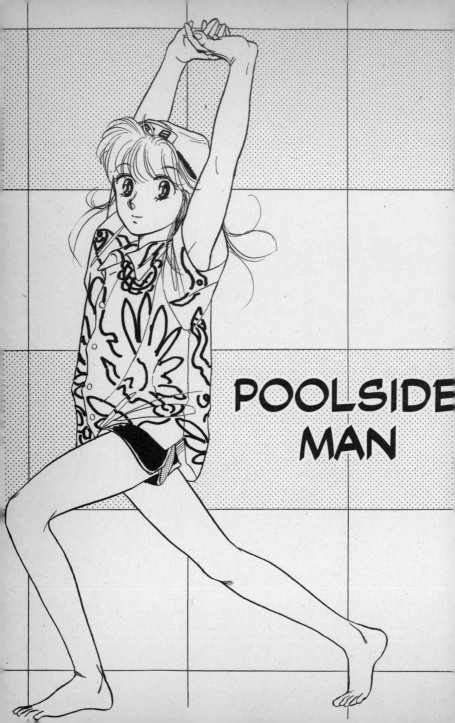

POOLSIDE
MAN

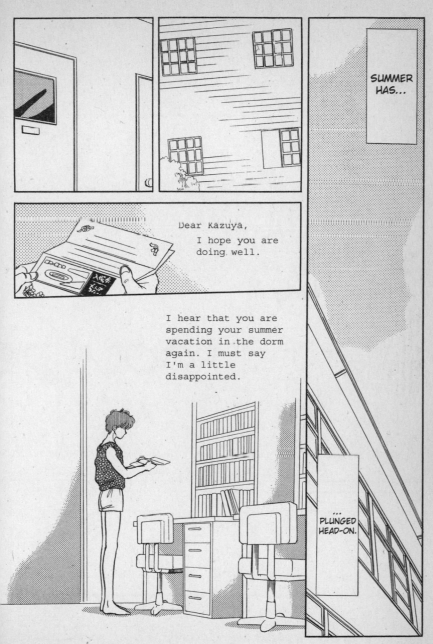

SUMMER HAS...
... PLUNGED HEAD-ON.
Dear Kazuya,
I hope you are doing well.
I hear that you are spending your summer vacation in the dorm again. I must say I'm a little disappointed.

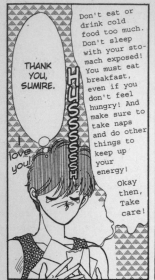

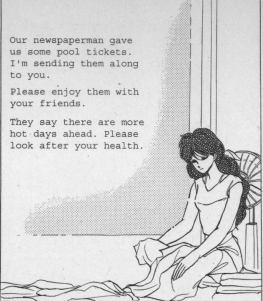

Our newspaperman gave us some pool tickets. I'm sending them along to you.
Please enjoy them with your friends.
They say there are more hot days ahead. Please look after your health.
Don't eat or drink cold food too much. Don't sleep with your stomach exposed! You must eat breakfast, even if you don't feel hungry! And make sure to take naps and do other things to keep up your energy!
Okay then, Take care!
HUSSSSSSH
THANK YOU, SUMIRE.
I love you!
I COUNT FOUR TICKETS.
I'M HEADING HOME TOMORROW!
YEAH, AND THE WEATHER'S GREAT TODAY!
LISTEN, YOU...
AND THUS, WE ALL WENT OFF TO THE POOL.

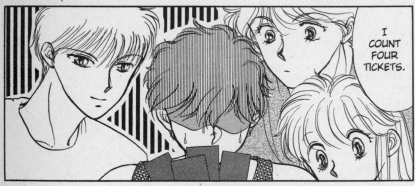

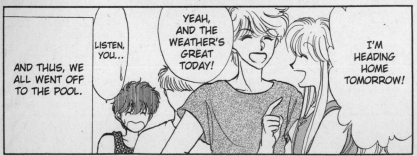

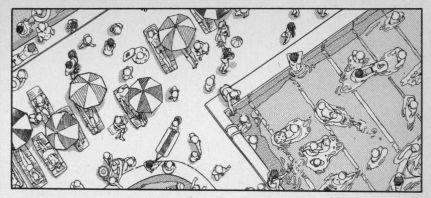

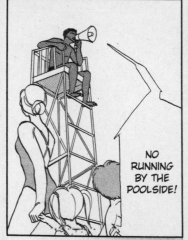

KYAA
KYAA
YOU—DOWN THERE!
LENON
NO RUNNING BY THE POOLSIDE!
TSK!

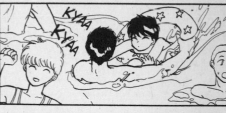

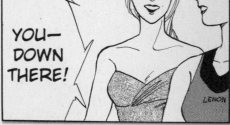

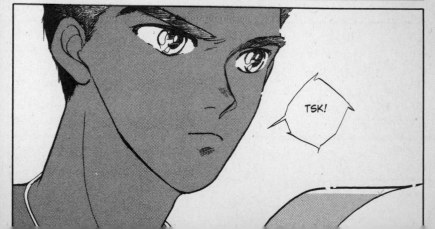

7 Poo
I WOULD NEVER COME TO A PLACE LIKE THIS UNLESS IT WAS FREE.
I WANTED IT TO BE A HOTEL POOL.
WHY SEVEN, I WONDER? IS THERE SOME ADVANTAGE?
EH?
IF YOU WOULD COME THIS WAY...
EXCUSE ME! EXCUSE ME!

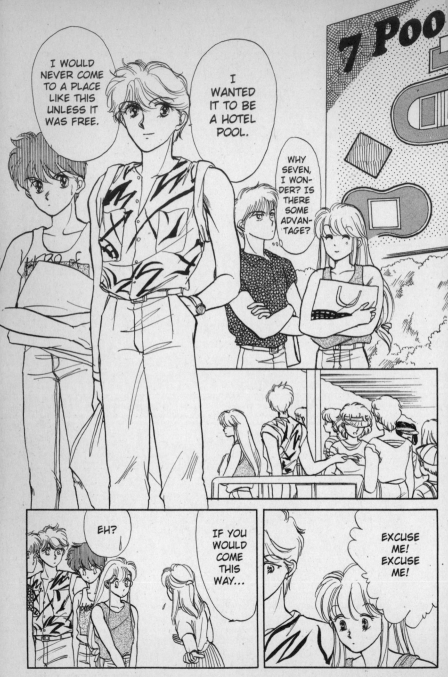

WOMEN'S CHANGING ROOMS
ENTRANCE
THE WOMEN'S CHANGING ROOMS ARE THIS WAY.
NERIMA
BUT, I'M...
YOU SHOULD CHANGE IN THESE ROOMS. THIS WAY, PLEASE.
NERIMAEN
WHAT A WEIRD GIRL!
LISTEN! YOU'VE GOT IT WRONG!
I'M *REALLY* NOT THE PERSON YOU THINK I--
NERIMEN
SEM-PAIIII!!
PUSH
GEEEH?!
EXIT
POOLS
RESTROOMS

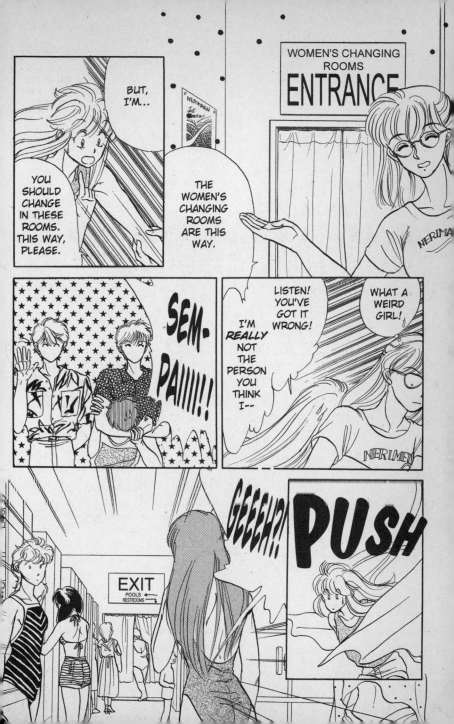

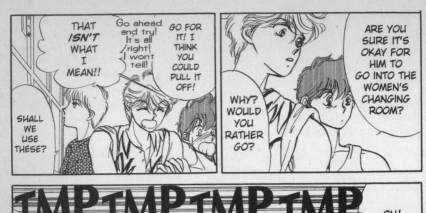

ARE YOU SURE IT'S OKAY FOR HIM TO GO INTO THE WOMEN'S CHANGING ROOM?
WHY? WOULD YOU RATHER GO?
GO FOR IT! I THINK YOU COULD PULL IT OFF!
Go ahead and try! It's all right! I won't tell!
THAT ISN'T WHAT I MEAN!!
SHALL WE USE THESE?
OH! LISTEN TO THAT RUNNING SPEED.
TMP TMP TMP TMP
WHOOSH
EXIT
POOLS
RESTROOMS
YOU MADE IT.
SEE ANYTHING GOOD?
GAMPH
?
Map
Women
Men
Exit
Entrance
This was the route he ran.

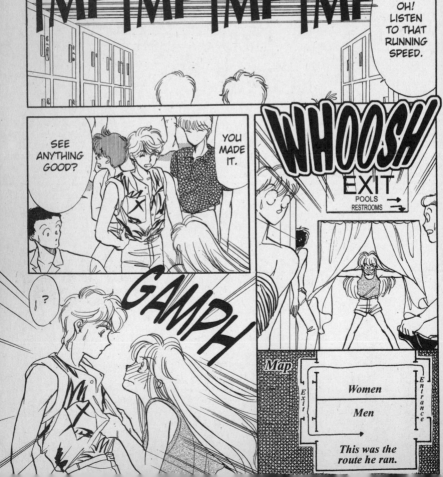

WHAAAAAA--?
?
WH-WHAT DID YOU JUST...
HUMPH! GOT HIM BACK!
HE REALLY IS A FULL-FLEDGED MAN!
You should learn from his style of revenge.
WOBBL WOBBL
SHUN, YOU SHOULD REST UP A BIT.
SO, WEAR THAT WHILE IT DRIES.
IT SHOULD DRY UP QUICK.
SO I'M A DRYING ROD, NOW?!
Washed

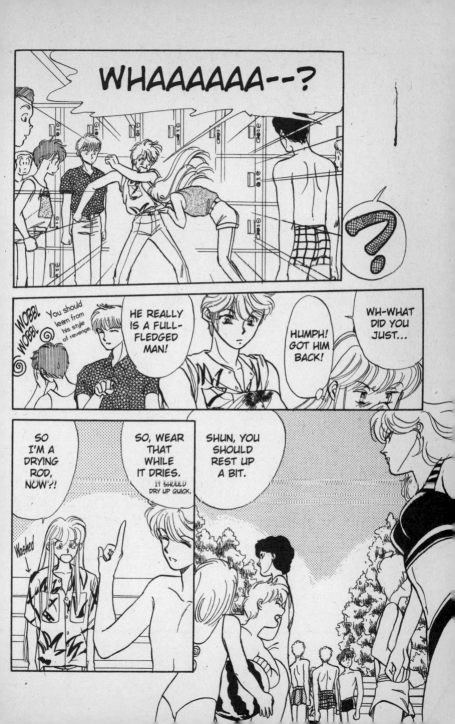

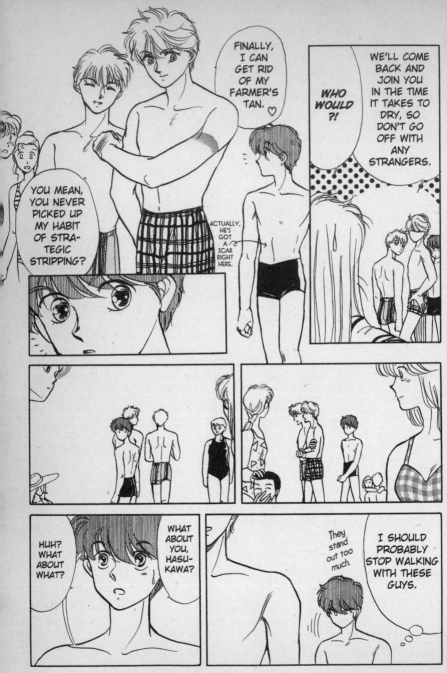

WE'LL COME BACK AND JOIN YOU IN THE TIME IT TAKES TO DRY, SO DON'T GO OFF WITH ANY STRANGERS.
WHO WOULD ?!
FINALLY, I CAN GET RID OF MY FARMER'S TAN. ♡
YOU MEAN, YOU NEVER PICKED UP MY HABIT OF STRA-TEGIC STRIPPING?
ACTUALLY, HE'S GOT A SCAR RIGHT HERE.
I SHOULD PROBABLY STOP WALKING WITH THESE GUYS.
They stand out too much.
WHAT ABOUT YOU, HASU-KAWA?
HUH? WHAT ABOUT WHAT?

I'M ASKING IF YOU CAN SWIM!
KICK
GABLOOSH
HEH HEH HEH
WHAT CAN WE DO WITH HIM?
WHEET-WHEEEEET
YOU, THERE!!
STOP THAT! YOU'RE PUTTING PEOPLE IN DANGER!
SOME PEOPLE!
TSK!
YOU JERKS SHOULD JUST STAY AT HOME! CAUSING ME TROUBLE!
HOW OLD ARE YOU, ANYWAY?

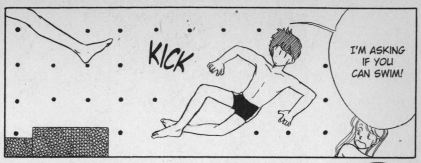

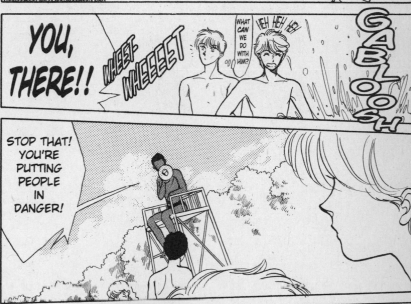

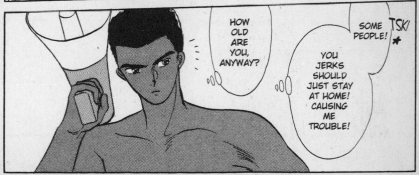

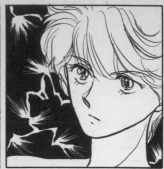

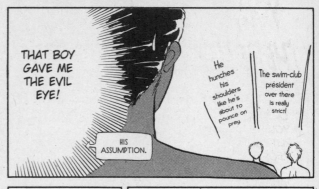

The swim-club president over there is really strict!
He hunches his shoulders like he's about to pounce on prey.
THAT BOY GAVE ME THE EVIL EYE!
HIS ASSUMPTION.
If I weren't able to swim, you'd be a criminal!
HA HA HA
THEN GO AHEAD AND DROWN! I WON'T SAVE YOU!
THIS MAN, (i), HAS A PART-TIME JOB AS A POOL LIFEGUARD.
AT 18-YEARS-OLD, AND A 1ST YEAR STUDENT IN COLLEGE, HE HOLDS A POSITION ON THE COLLEGE SWIM TEAM.
FOR GOD'S SAKE!

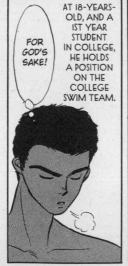

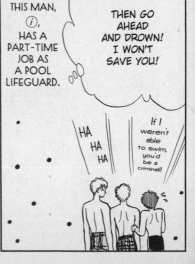

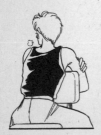

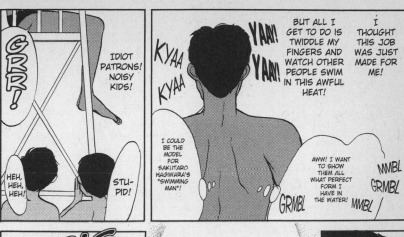

I THOUGHT THIS JOB WAS JUST MADE FOR ME!
BUT ALL I GET TO DO IS TWIDDLE MY FINGERS AND WATCH OTHER PEOPLE SWIM IN THIS AWFUL HEAT!
YAAY! YAAY!
KYAA KYAA
I COULD BE THE MODEL FOR SAKUTARO HAGIWARA'S "SWIMMING MAN"!
AWW! I WANT TO SHOW THEM ALL WHAT PERFECT FORM I HAVE IN THE WATER!
MMBL GRMBL
GRMBL MMBL
IDIOT PATRONS! NOISY KIDS!
GRR!
STU-PID!
HEH, HEH, HEH!
SHE'S CUTE! JUST MY TYPE!

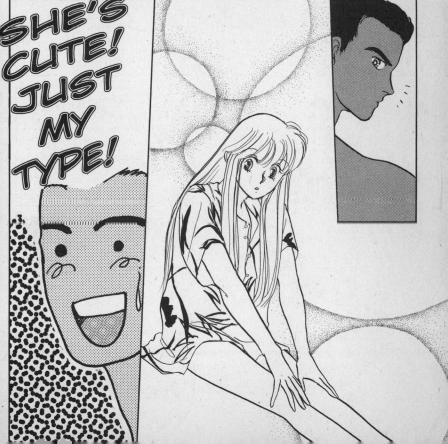

THIN LEGS, RUSTLING LONG HAIR, SKIN SO FAIR IT'S ALMOST A SHAME TO TAN IT IN THE SUN!
SEE? SO THIN!
WHEN DID SHE GET HERE? JUST SEVERAL METERS AWAY!
.....
I DON'T SEE ANYBODY WITH HER.
HMMMMMM
IT'S SO HOT!
WAVE WAVE
Isn't it nice of the pretty lady to wave at you?

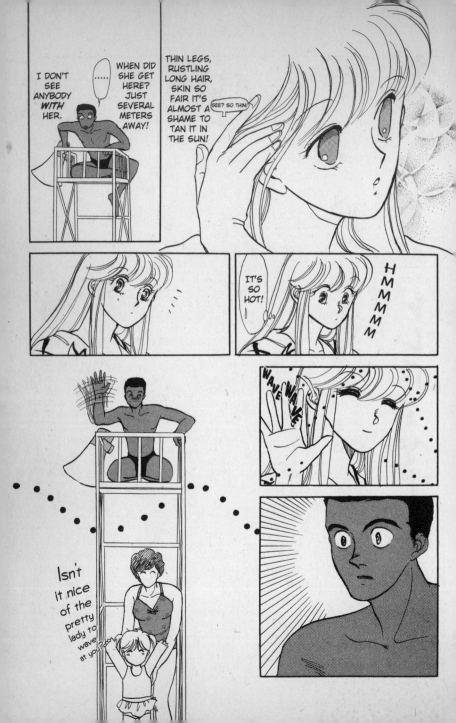

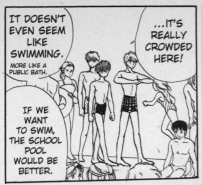

IT DOESN'T EVEN SEEM LIKE SWIMMING.
MORE LIKE A PUBLIC BATH.
...IT'S REALLY CROWDED HERE!
IF WE WANT TO SWIM, THE SCHOOL POOL WOULD BE BETTER.
I HAVE TO SAY...
BOING
THEN WHAT DID WE COME HERE FOR?
SORRY AGAIN!
Thanks!
See ya!
I'M SO SORRY!
WHAT'S THAT?
IS THAT WHAT YOU CAME TO SEE?
BECAUSE THERE ARE SOME FUNDAMENTAL DIFFERENCES BETWEEN THIS AND THE SCHOOL POOL.

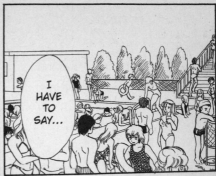

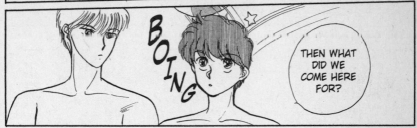

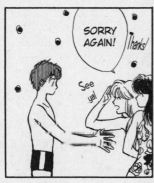

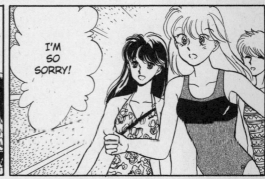

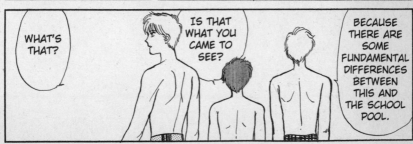

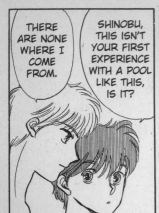

A WAVE POOL.
SHINOBU, THIS ISN'T YOUR FIRST EXPERIENCE WITH A POOL LIKE THIS, IS IT?
THERE ARE NONE WHERE I COME FROM.
IT GETS DEEP QUICKLY, DOESN'T IT?
SHF
THAT'S RIGHT. ONLY MITSURU AND I ARE FROM THE CITY.
SLOOSH
IT'S DANGEROUS...
...FOR A GIRL THAT CUTE TO BE ALONE.
SOME SEX-CRAZED CREEP COULD COME OUT OF NOWHERE!
SOMEONE HAD BETTER KEEP AN EYE ON HER.

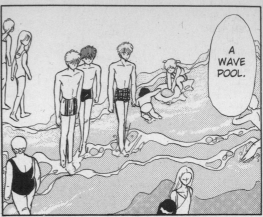

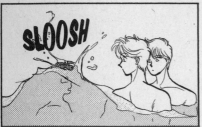

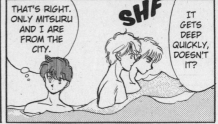

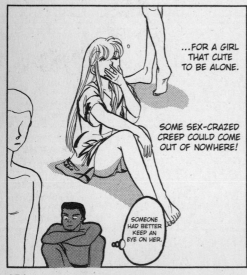

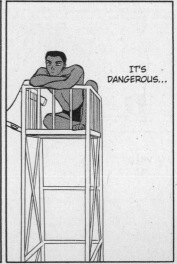

AWW! I WANT TO LEAVE THIS STUPID LIFEGUARD TOWER BEHIND AND BRING THAT CREEP DOWN!
WHAT SCHOOL DO YOU GO TO?
HEY! ARE YOU ALONE?
What's with him?
RYOKUTO ACADEMY. WHY?
THERE'S ONE ALREADY! DAMMIT!
HUH? WHAT?
THAT'S FUNNY! ISN'T THAT SUPPOSED TO BE A BOYS' SCHOOL?
LOOK.

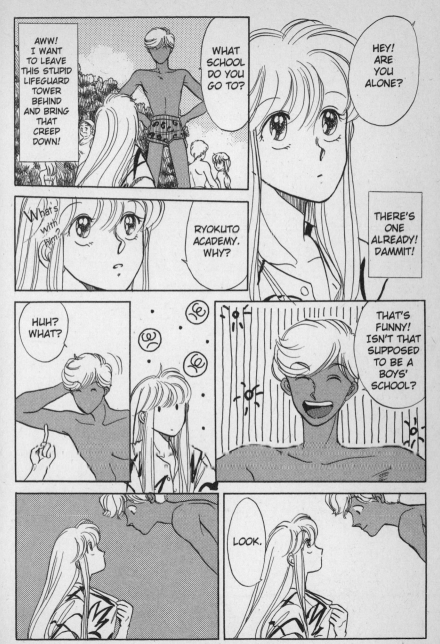

OOHH! I SHOULD NEVER HAVE LOOKED!
HA! SHE CHASED HIM OFF!
TAKE THAT, CREEP!
BESIDES, POOLS AREN'T FOR ANYTHING BUT SWIMMING!
YEP! YEP!
IT ISN'T FOR EATING, DRINKING, OR PICKING UP GIRLS!
5 m
HASUKAWA, GIVE US A BACKWARDS SOMERSAULT!
OOOH!
KABLOOP

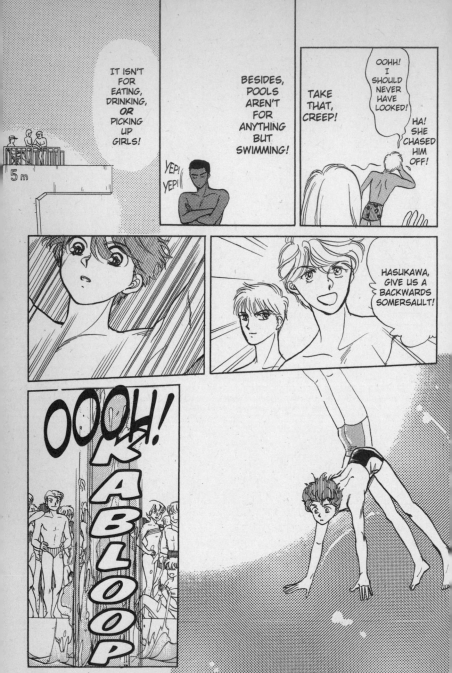

I- IT'S SO DEEP!
GURBL GURBL
DEPTH: 5 METERS.
BLOOSH
HAAH HAAH
HUH?
WHERE'S MITSURU?
WHY? WHY'S HE SUCH A LADIES MAN?!
SORRY, I'M LATE. I WAS BEING *PICKED UP BY SOME GIRLS.*
WHAT'S SO UNUSUAL ABOUT THAT?!
AWW! IT'S EMBARRASSING!
MITSURU, DON'T YOU THINK THAT SHUN WOULD START GETTING ANTSY RIGHT ABOUT NOW?
KYAA!
OH, I GUESS SO.
LET'S GO GET HIM.

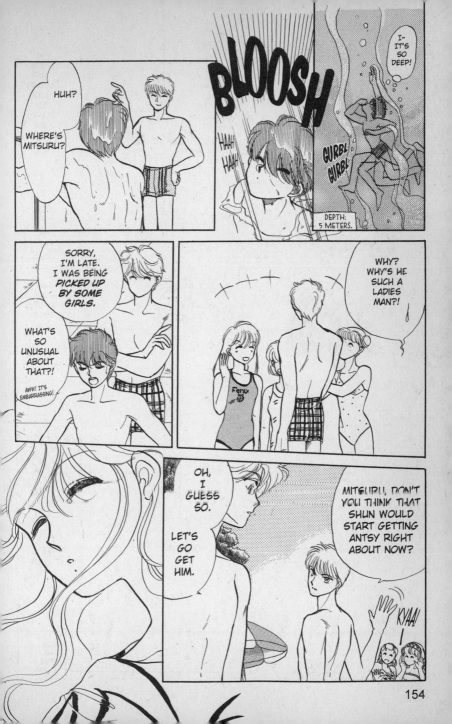

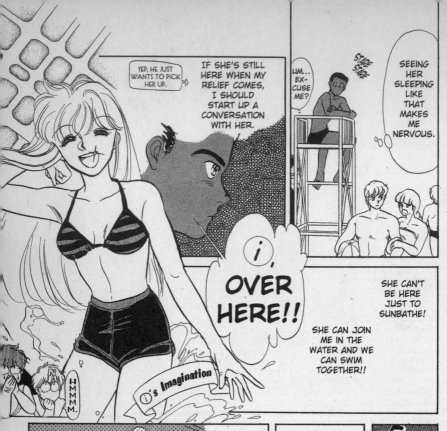

SEEING HER SLEEPING LIKE THAT MAKES ME NERVOUS.
STARE STARE
UM... EX-CUSE ME?
IF SHE'S STILL HERE WHEN MY RELIEF COMES, I SHOULD START UP A CONVERSATION WITH HER.
YEP, HE JUST WANTS TO PICK HER UP.
SHE CAN'T BE HERE JUST TO SUNBATHE!
SHE CAN JOIN ME IN THE WATER AND WE CAN SWIM TOGETHER!!
i, OVER HERE!!
i's Imagination
HMMMM.
EH-HEH
FOR THE THIRD TIME, WHERE IS THE FRIGGIN' RESTROOM?!
WHAT'S THIS?
HEY!
SHUUUN!
IT'S THAT INSOLENT BRAT AGAIN!

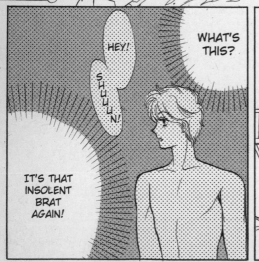

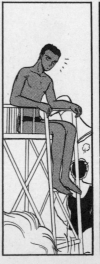

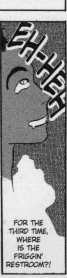

I KNEW IT! HIS FACE JUST SCREAMS THAT HE'S TRYING TO PICK UP WOMEN!
AND HE SURE FOUND HER FAST, DIDN'T HE?
DON'T EVEN GET CLOSE, YOU PERVERT!
HEY! WHAT ARE YOU DOING?
HE'S SLEEP-ING.
I GUESS IT'S DRY.
BONNG
YOU PERV! YOU'LL REGRET THAT!
KYAA!
THAT CHILD IS STRUG-GLING!
NO! I'M THE ONLY ONE WHO SEES IT!

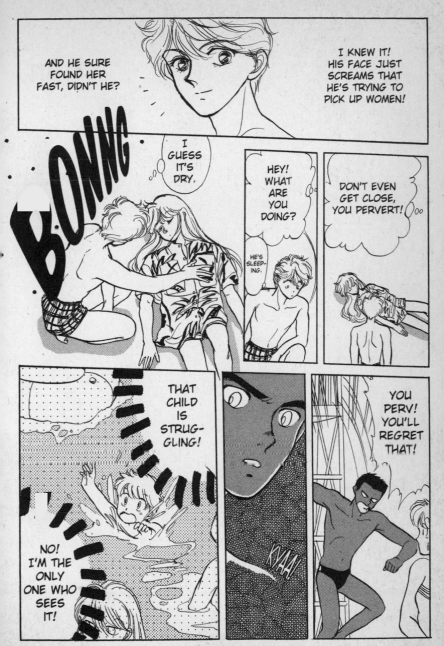

DAMMIT!
IF I LEAVE HER, SHE'LL BE IN DANGER!
BUT I CAN'T LET THE KID TO DROWN EITHER!
GLUB
GLUB
GLUB
GLUB
GLUB
BLUB
BOTH SCENARIOS PLAY OUT IN HIS IMAGINATION.
OH, HELL!

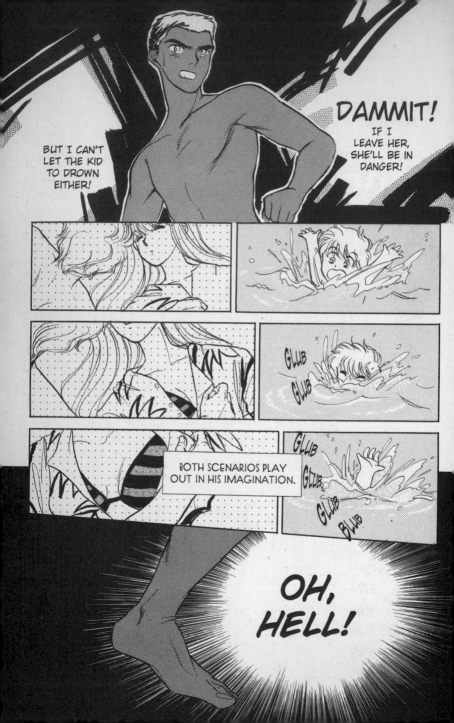

MY DUTY AS A LIFE-GUARD MUST COME FIRST!!
Of course it does!!
Hurry up and save me!
SPORSH
THANK YOU SO MUCH! I DON'T KNOW WHAT I CAN DO TO THANK YOU!
NO, I'M JUST GLAD I NOTICED HIM. THE ONLY IMPORTANT THING IS THAT HE'S OKAY.
NICELY DONE, (i)
(i)?
THE GIRL? IS THE GIRL OKAY?
KLAP KLAP KLAP

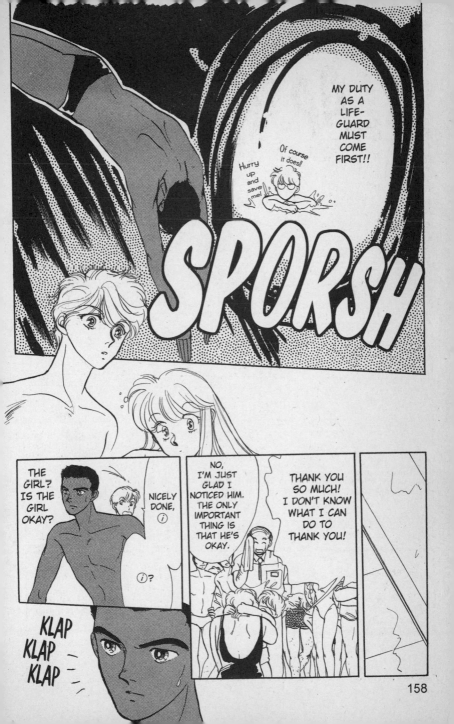

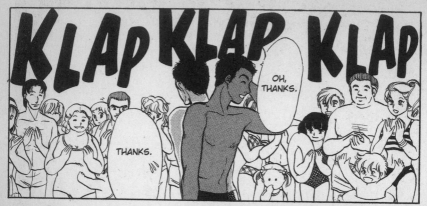

KLAP KLAP KLAP

OH, THANKS.

THANKS.

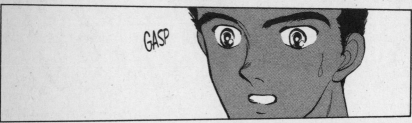

GASP

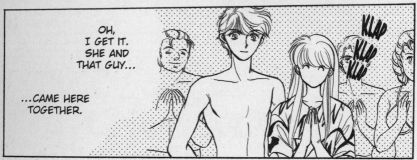

OH, I GET IT. SHE AND THAT GUY...

...CAME HERE TOGETHER.

KLAP KLAP KLAP

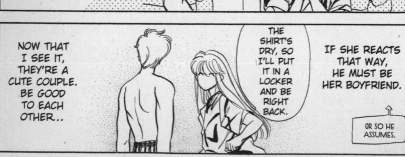

NOW THAT I SEE IT, THEY'RE A CUTE COUPLE. BE GOOD TO EACH OTHER...

THE SHIRT'S DRY, SO I'LL PUT IT IN A LOCKER AND BE RIGHT BACK.

IF SHE REACTS THAT WAY, HE MUST BE HER BOYFRIEND.

OR SO HE ASSUMES.

AND AS FOR ME, I'LL NEVER LET MY ATTENTION WANDER AGAIN.
I LIVE BY THE VIRTUE OF THE LIFE-GUARD!
HEY, ⓘ! ⓘ!!
HEH
TODAY WAS A REVELATION OF THE GODS!
SHE WAS MY HEAVENLY MESSENGER.
NOW...
...MY LIFEGUARD TOWER AWAITS ME.
HE MAY BE A LITTLE EXTREME, BUT THERE-AFTER...
SUKA-CHAN!!
REALITY
DIZZ DIZZ
Don't get too close!
What's wrong with you?!
...IT ONLY TOOK ANOTHER FIVE MINUTES FOR REALITY TO SMACK HIM ON THE HEAD.

POOLSIDE MAN: THE END

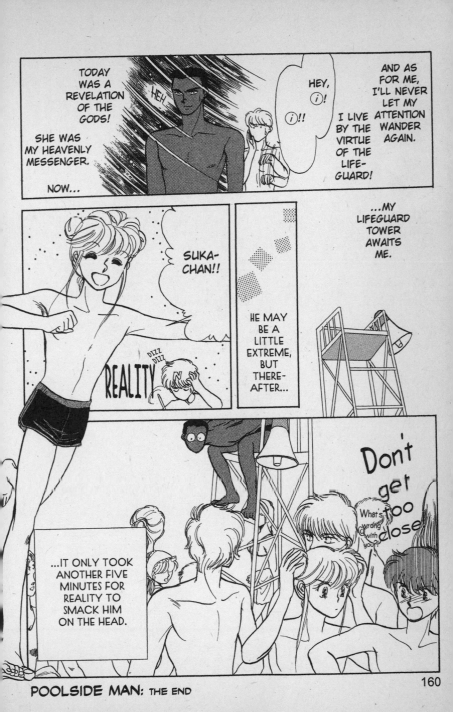

THE
TRUE LOVE
OF A
BROTHER

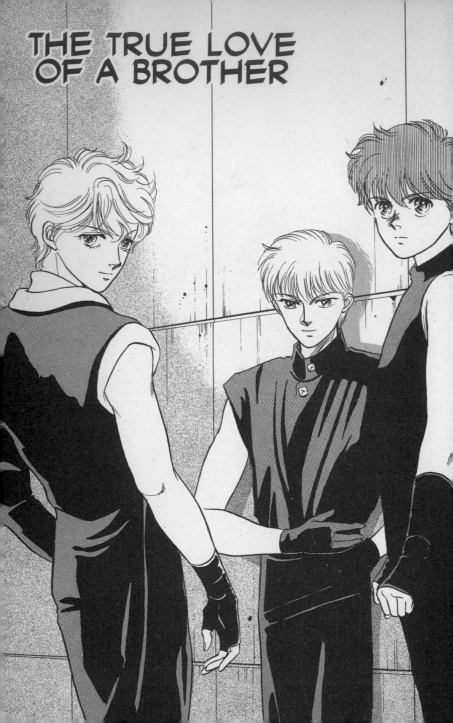

THE TRUE LOVE
OF A BROTHER

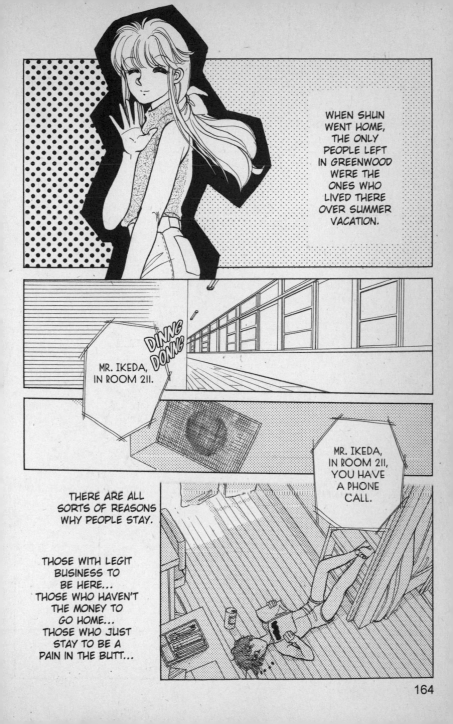

WHEN SHUN WENT HOME, THE ONLY PEOPLE LEFT IN GREENWOOD WERE THE ONES WHO LIVED THERE OVER SUMMER VACATION.

DINNG DONNG

MR. IKEDA, IN ROOM 211.

MR. IKEDA, IN ROOM 211, YOU HAVE A PHONE CALL.

THERE ARE ALL SORTS OF REASONS WHY PEOPLE STAY.

THOSE WITH LEGIT BUSINESS TO BE HERE... THOSE WHO HAVEN'T THE MONEY TO GO HOME... THOSE WHO JUST STAY TO BE A PAIN IN THE BUTT...

164

THOSE WHO CAN'T GO HOME... THOSE WHO *DON'T WANT* TO GO HOME...
Office
HELLO ?
YEAH.
ARE *YOU* DOING OKAY?
...YEAH.
YEAH, I GOT IT.
UH-HUH.
SEE YOU.
THANK YOU.
KACHAK
HUH?
YOU'RE GOING HOME?

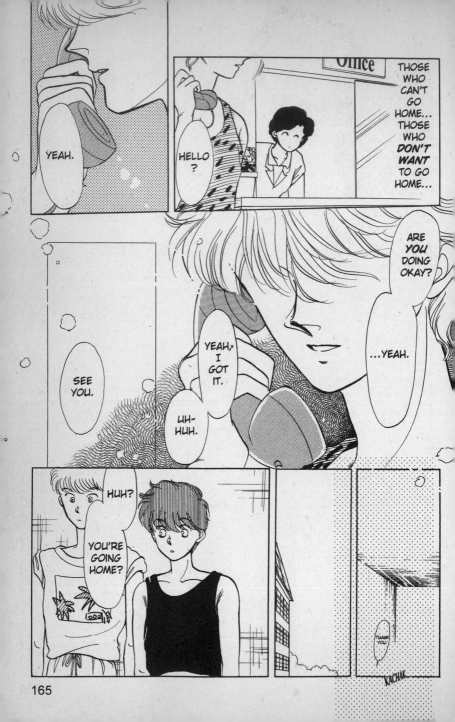

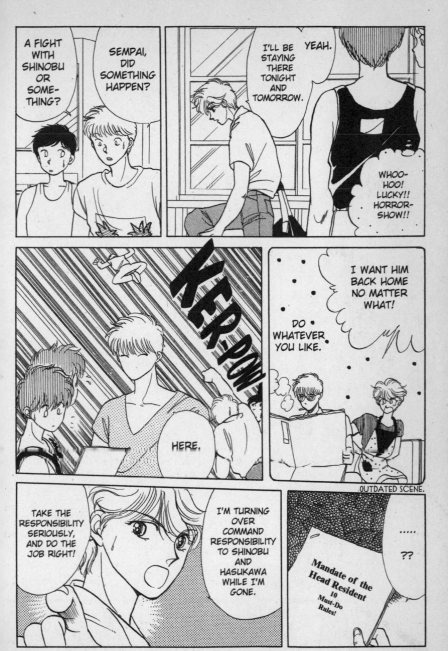

YEAH.
I'LL BE STAYING THERE TONIGHT AND TOMORROW.
WHOO-HOO! LUCKY!! HORROR-SHOW!!
SEMPAI, DID SOMETHING HAPPEN?
A FIGHT WITH SHINOBU OR SOME-THING?
I WANT HIM BACK HOME NO MATTER WHAT!
DO WHATEVER YOU LIKE.
OUTDATED SCENE.
KER-POW
HERE.
.....
??
Mandate of the Head Resident 10 Must-Do Rules!
I'M TURNING OVER COMMAND RESPONSIBILITY TO SHINOBU AND HASUKAWA WHILE I'M GONE.
TAKE THE RESPONSIBILITY SERIOUSLY, AND DO THE JOB RIGHT!

WE'RE THE SUBSTITUTE HEAD RESIDENTS? SHINOBU AND I?
I DON'T WANNA!
DID YOU JUST SAY, ***"I DON'T WANNA"***?!
I ***DIDN'T*** SAY IT!
I'LL SEE YOU GUYS.
TAKE CARE OF THINGS.
WHY?!
IF YOU'RE COMING BACK ANYWAY, WHY DIDN'T YOU JUST GO HOME FOR A VACATION?

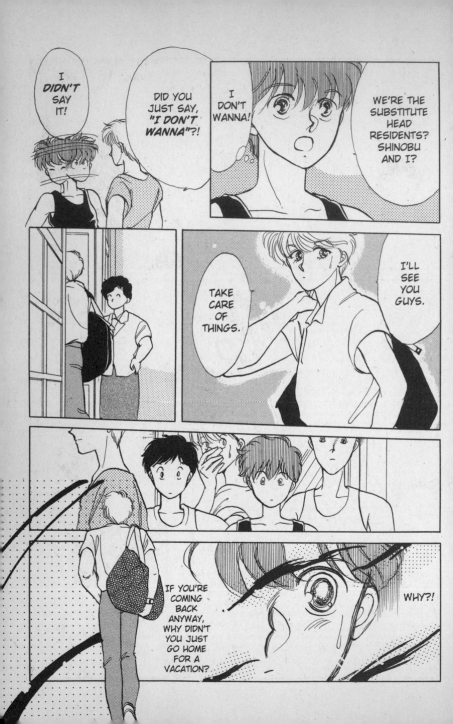

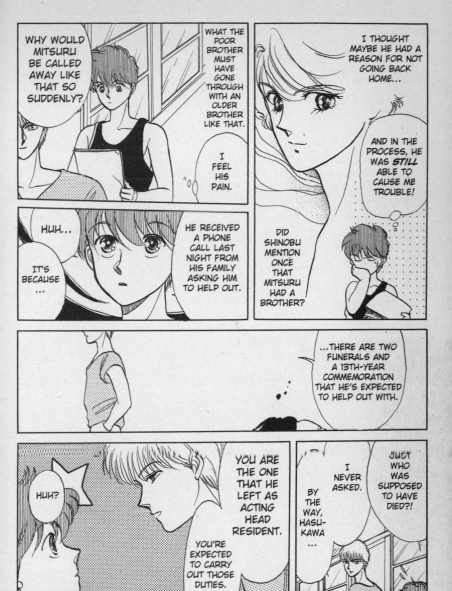

WHY WOULD MITSURU BE CALLED AWAY LIKE THAT SO SUDDENLY?
WHAT THE POOR BROTHER MUST HAVE GONE THROUGH WITH AN OLDER BROTHER LIKE THAT.
I FEEL HIS PAIN.
HUH...
IT'S BECAUSE ...
HE RECEIVED A PHONE CALL LAST NIGHT FROM HIS FAMILY ASKING HIM TO HELP OUT.
I THOUGHT MAYBE HE HAD A REASON FOR NOT GOING BACK HOME...
AND IN THE PROCESS, HE WAS **STILL** ABLE TO CAUSE ME TROUBLE!
DID SHINOBU MENTION ONCE THAT MITSURU HAD A BROTHER?
...THERE ARE TWO FUNERALS AND A 13TH-YEAR COMMEMORATION THAT HE'S EXPECTED TO HELP OUT WITH.
HUH?
YOU ARE THE ONE THAT HE LEFT AS ACTING HEAD RESIDENT.
YOU'RE EXPECTED TO CARRY OUT THOSE DUTIES.
BY THE WAY, HASU-KAWA ...
I NEVER ASKED.
JUST WHO WAS SUPPOSED TO HAVE DIED?!

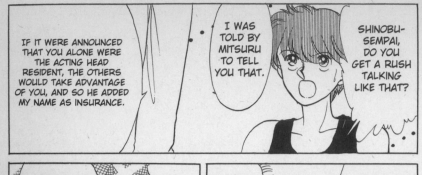

SHINOBU-SEMPAI, DO YOU GET A RUSH TALKING LIKE THAT?
I WAS TOLD BY MITSURU TO TELL YOU THAT.
IF IT WERE ANNOUNCED THAT YOU ALONE WERE THE ACTING HEAD RESIDENT, THE OTHERS WOULD TAKE ADVANTAGE OF YOU, AND SO HE ADDED MY NAME AS INSURANCE.
OF COURSE, IF YOU GET IN TROUBLE, HE ALSO ASKED ME TO COME TO YOUR AID, BUT...
... OTHER THAN THAT, THE JOB IS YOURS ALONE.
YOU'RE KIDDING!
HE'S ALREADY FINGERED YOU AS THE MOST LIKELY CANDIDATE FOR THE NEXT HEAD RESIDENT.
SO PERFORM YOUR DUTIES ACCORDINGLY.
YOU'VE BEEN ENTRUSTED WITH A GRAVE RESPONSIBILITY. DON'T BETRAY THAT TRUST.
WHAAAAAA--?!
OH, COME ON!
ASK ME BEFORE YOU TRUST ME, OKAY?!
WAKE UP AND SMELL THE CAT!
HEAD RESIDENT?
SMELLY CAT

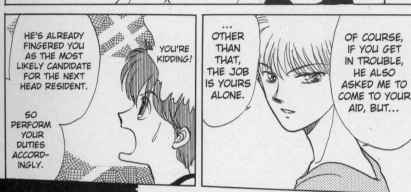

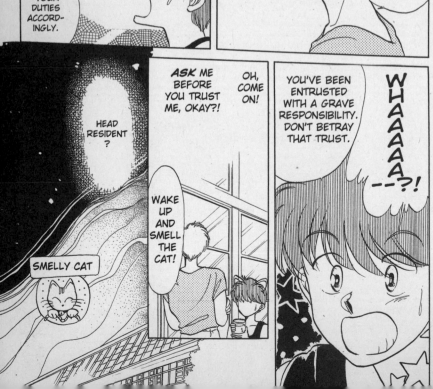

SKUFF
TMp TMp
THIS IS IT!

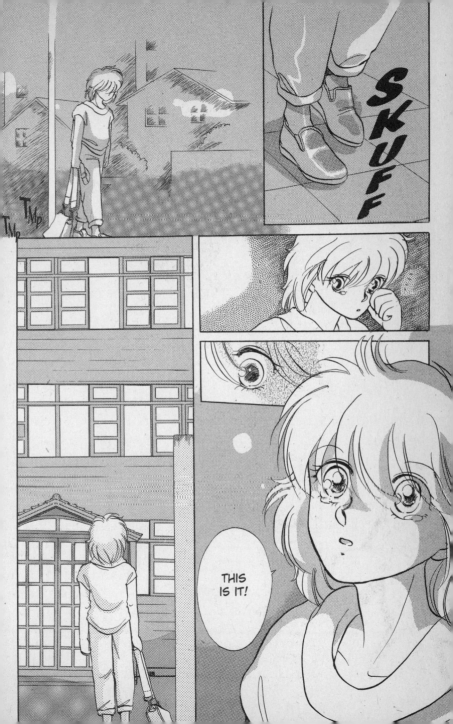

WHAT? ARE YOU STILL CLEANING?
BUT IT'S ALMOST 10 P.M.
THE JOB OF A HEAD RESIDENT IS ACTUALLY...
WHO CARES *WHEN* I CLEAN UP?
SO LONG AS I DO IT SOMETIME TODAY, RIGHT?
THAT'S TRUE, BUT...
LOOK AT YOU—BEING ACTING HEAD RESIDENT WHILE MITSURU'S AWAY!
OH, SHUT UP.
HEY, SINCE THERE ARE SO FEW PEOPLE HERE, WHY DON'T YOU ORDER EVERYBODY TO USE ONLY THE FIRST FLOOR BATHROOM!
IT'LL MAKE CLEANING SO MUCH EASIER!
WHO WOULD FOLLOW AN ORDER LIKE THAT?!
...WELL, ASIDE FROM KEEPING TROUBLE-MAKERS IN CHECK, IT'S ONLY FOLLOWING-UP ON CLEANING AND THE LIGHTS-OUT CHECK.

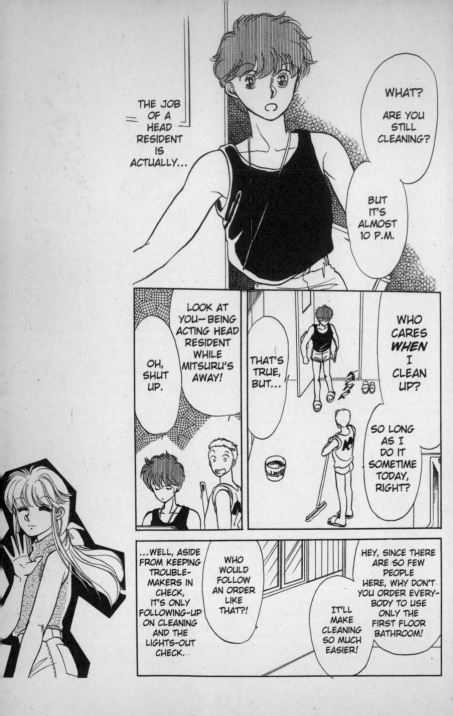

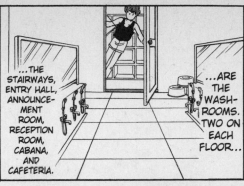

...THE STAIRWAYS, ENTRY HALL, ANNOUNCEMENT ROOM, RECEPTION ROOM, CABANA, AND CAFETERIA.

...ARE THE WASHROOMS. TWO ON EACH FLOOR...

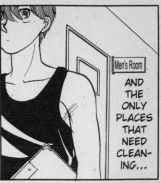

AND THE ONLY PLACES THAT NEED CLEANING...

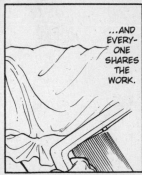

...AND EVERYONE SHARES THE WORK.

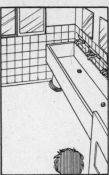

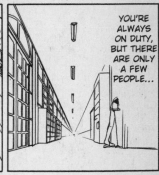

YOU'RE ALWAYS ON DUTY, BUT THERE ARE ONLY A FEW PEOPLE...

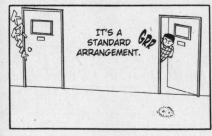

IT'S A STANDARD ARRANGEMENT.

GRR

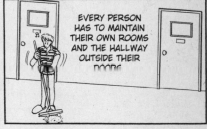

EVERY PERSON HAS TO MAINTAIN THEIR OWN ROOMS AND THE HALLWAY OUTSIDE THEIR DOORS.

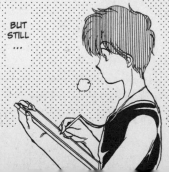

WALKING FROM ONE END TO ANOTHER, YOU REALLY SEE JUST HOW BIG THIS SPACE IS.

BUT STILL...

SO ALL I HAVE LEFT TO DO IS THE LIGHTS-OUT CHECK!
COME TO THINK OF IT, THE HEAD RESIDENT IS LIKE BEING AN ADMINISTRATIVE HANDYMAN!
THIS IS EASY! ♡
OH! PERFECT TIMING, MR. HASUKAWA!
IT IS?
TMP TMP
I KNOW YOU'RE ONLY A SUBSTITUTE, SO I'M SORRY ABOUT THIS...
SOMETHING SUDDENLY CAME UP, AND I HAVE TO LEAVE!
I'LL BE BACK TONIGHT. YOU CAN HANDLE THINGS UNTIL THEN, CAN'T YOU?
S-SURE...
IT SHOULD BE OKAY, RIGHT? THERE WOULDN'T BE ANYONE COMING TO VISIT THIS LATE.
THIS IS AWFUL! I HAVE SO MUCH TO DO!

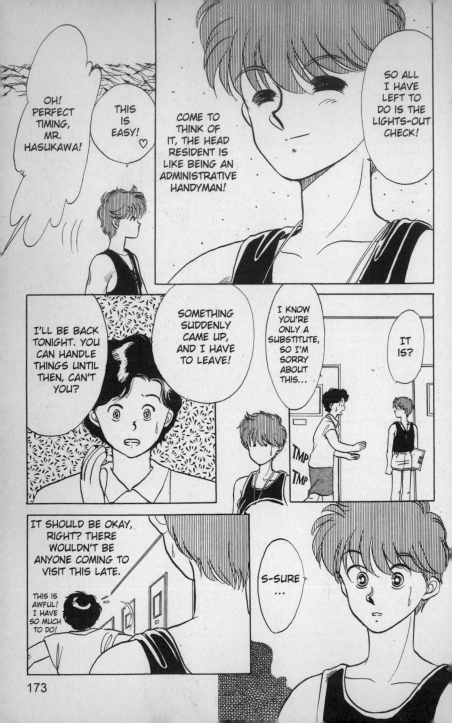

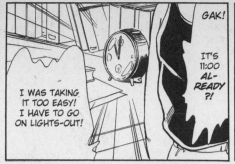

GAK!
IT'S 11:00 AL-READY ?!
I WAS TAKING IT TOO EASY! I HAVE TO GO ON LIGHTS-OUT!
210
I GUESS THERE ARE A LOT OF THINGS THAT CAN HAPPEN IN A DORM.
.....
WHAT TO DO IF A GH
APPEARS
1. Ignore it
2. Run away screaming
3. Reason with it
4. Pray for its redemptio
*All apparitions that appear outsi
building must absolutely be ignor
WH— WHAT IS THIS?!
Lights Out Check
1. Show no mercy
2. Use authority and vio
to cow them
3. Accept bribes of cash o
goods
4. Do not allow yourself t
get waylaid(be especiall
wary of delay tactics)
IS THIS SERIOUS?!
.....
ONE MAY APPEAR, YOU KNOW.

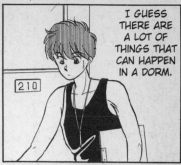

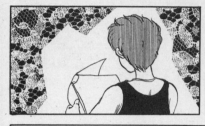

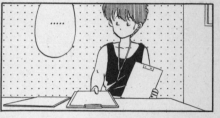

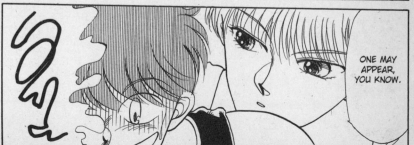

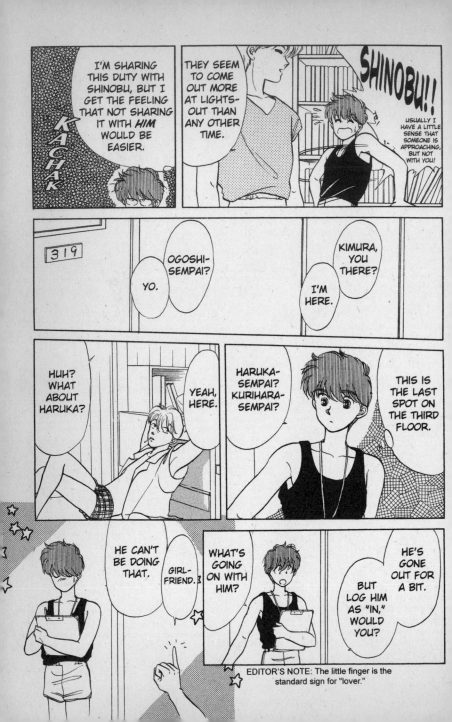

SHINOBU!!
USUALLY I HAVE A LITTLE SENSE THAT SOMEONE IS APPROACHING, BUT NOT WITH YOU!
THEY SEEM TO COME OUT MORE AT LIGHTS-OUT THAN ANY OTHER TIME.
I'M SHARING THIS DUTY WITH SHINOBU, BUT I GET THE FEELING THAT NOT SHARING IT WITH *HIM* WOULD BE EASIER.
KACHAK
KIMURA, YOU THERE?
I'M HERE.
319
OGOSHI-SEMPAI?
YO.
THIS IS THE LAST SPOT ON THE THIRD FLOOR.
HARUKA-SEMPAI? KURIHARA-SEMPAI?
YEAH, HERE.
HUH? WHAT ABOUT HARUKA?
HE'S GONE OUT FOR A BIT.
BUT LOG HIM AS "IN," WOULD YOU?
WHAT'S GOING ON WITH HIM?
GIRL-FRIEND.
HE CAN'T BE DOING THAT.

EDITOR'S NOTE: The little finger is the standard sign for "lover."

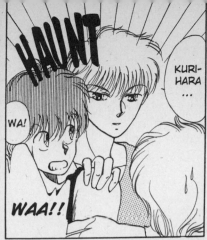

HAUNT
KURIHARA...
WA!
WAA!!
DON'T YOU HAVE ENOUGH RESPECT TO DO AS A SEMPAI DICTATES?
HEY, I CAN'T GIVE WHAT I—
I'M SORRY, HASUKAWA!
O-O-OKAY!
HASUKAWA HAS A TRICKY DUTY FILLING IN FOR MITSURU.
YOU SHOULDN'T FORCE HARD CHOICES ON HIM.
HE'S PAID INFORMERS TO TELL HIM NEARLY EVERY DORM RESIDENT'S WEAKNESSES.
WHY'S EVERYONE SO AFRAID OF SHINOBU-SEMPAI?
IF HE'S GOING TO FOLLOW ME, HE COULD DO THE JOB HIMSELF!
AND SO, GIVE IT YOUR BEST.

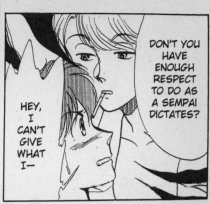

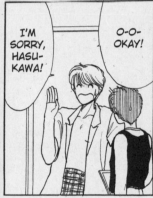

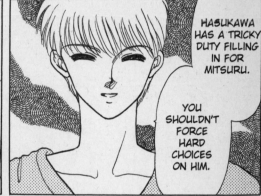

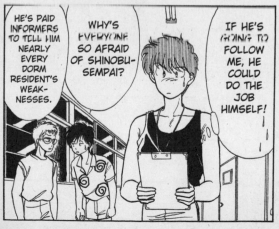

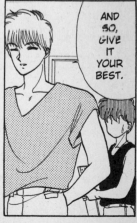

2ND FLOOR.
1ST FLOOR ... ... AND ...
IF MITSURU CAN DO IT, THEN I SHOULD BE ABLE TO...
MY JOB IS DONE!
KATAK
124
A NOISE CAME FROM OVER HERE, RIGHT?
BUT BOTH THE GUYS IN THIS ROOM WENT HOME.

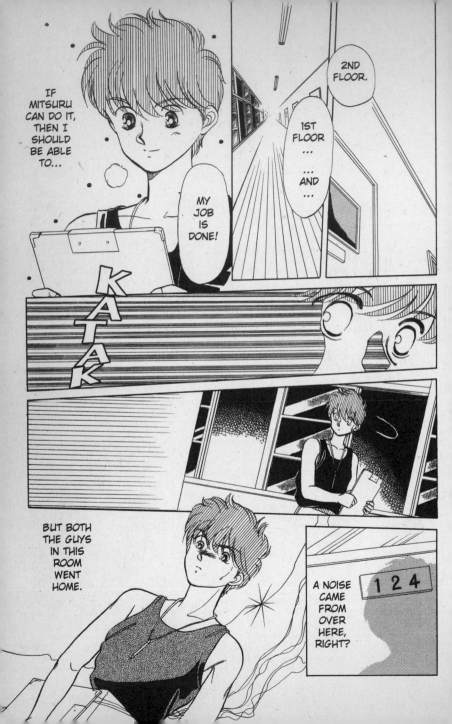

"ONE MAY APPEAR."
NO NO NO
THEY MAY HAVE LEFT A WIN-DOW OPEN ... MAYBE A CAT GOT IN ...
SST
A BURG-LAR?
ANYWAY, THERE'S NO NEED TO BE AFRAID OF GHOSTS.
BAM
WHO'S IN THERE?!

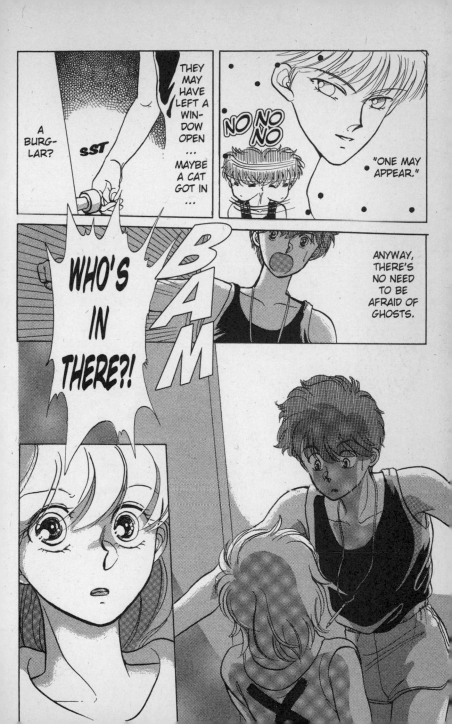

AAH!!
THMP
WHAT WAS THAT? A LITTLE GIRL?
WAIT!!
HMM?
TMP TMP TMP TMP
WHAT DO I DO?

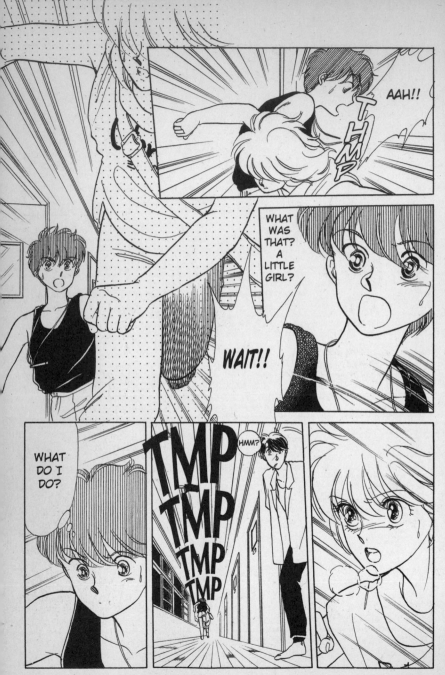

OH!
AH!
HOW CAN I HOLD HER DOWN WITHOUT BEING A PERVERT?
HUFF
HUFF
WHEEZE WHEEZE
WHO'S THE KID?
I CHECKED OUT AN EMPTY ROOM, AND THIS ONE CAME OUT.
WHAT IS THIS?
SHINOBU-SEMPAI!
WAAAHH!

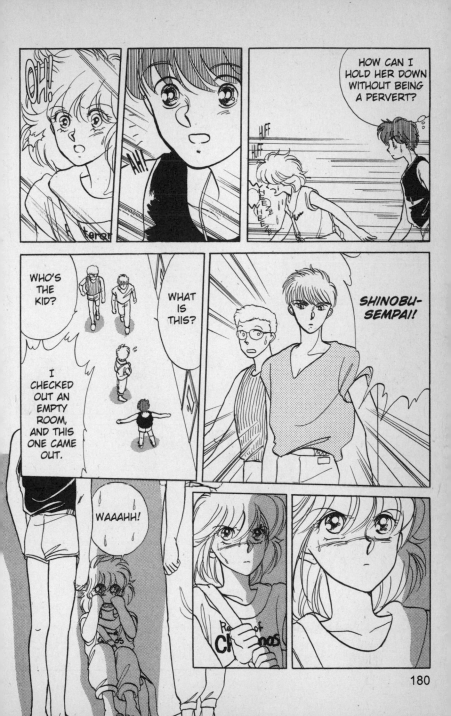

WHAT DID THE GIRLS OF THAT MIDDLE SCHOOL TELL YOU?
WHAT— AGAIN?
Reception Room.
A LITTLE GIRL HIDING IN THE DORM?
I SEE. IN ANY CASE, WE SHOULD PHONE HER HOME AND HAVE SOMEONE PICK HER UP.
THE DORM MOTHER?
NOT BACK YET.
THIS IS YOUR FAULT, RIGHT? TELL ME YOUR NUMBER.
WHAT'S WRONG WITH YOU?
WE WON'T SAY ANYTHING BAD ABOUT YOU.
HEY. WE'RE GONNA CALL YOUR MOMMY FOR YOU.
WHAT'S YOUR NUMBER?

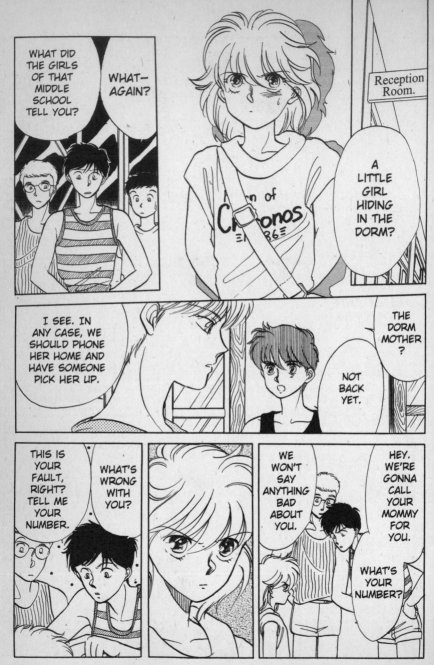

DON'T BE THAT WAY!
WE'RE TRYING TO HELP YOU GET HOME.
EVEN THOUGH IT'S A PAIN FOR US.
CALM DOWN.
YOU LITTLE BRAT!!
THBTZZ
I USED UP ALL MY MONEY, SO I CAN'T GO HOME!
I'M NOT GOING HOME !!
YOU'RE A RUNAWAY.
YOU MEAN SHE'S NOT FROM THAT NEARBY MIDDLE SCHOOL ?
WAIT...
YOUR MONEY ... TRAIN FARE?

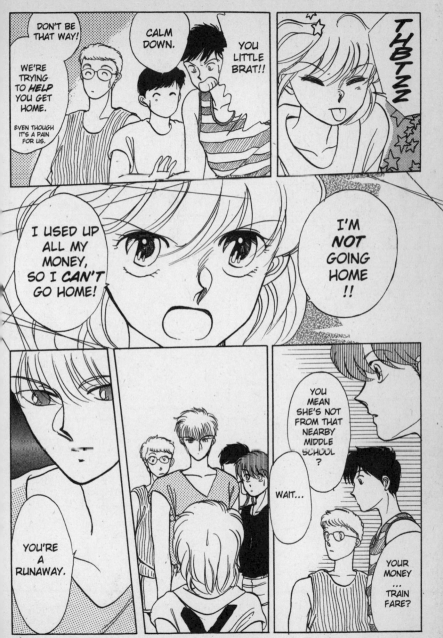

URK!
NOD
BIG PROBLEM
WHAT DO WE DO, SEMPAI?
WE CALL THE POLICE IS WHAT!
IN ANY CASE, WE'LL LET HER STAY HERE. SHE DIDN'T HAVE ANY PLACE TO SLEEP, AND THAT'S WHY SHE CLIMBED IN HERE, RIGHT?
LET HER STAY? WHERE?
CAN WE DO THAT?
WELL, ONLY UNTIL THE DORM MOTHER GETS BACK.
SO UNTIL SHE DOES ...
HASU-KAWA?
YEAH?
SHE'S YOUR RESPON-SIBILITY, SO BE A GOOD GUARDIAN.
EH?

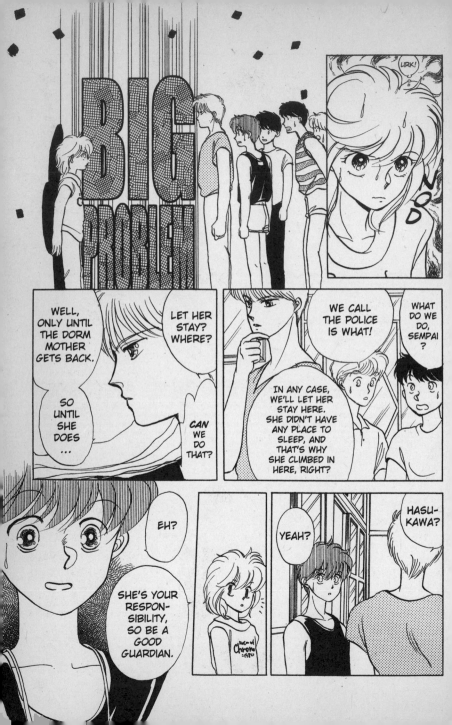

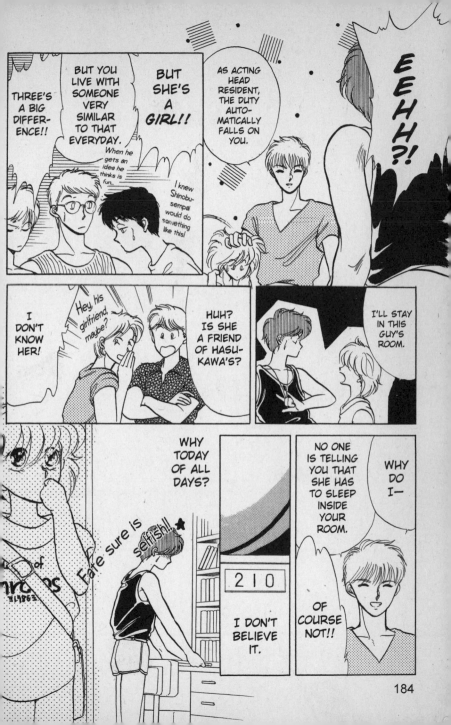

EEHH?!
AS ACTING HEAD RESIDENT, THE DUTY AUTO-MATICALLY FALLS ON YOU.
I knew Shinobu-sempai would do something like this!
BUT SHE'S A GIRL!!
BUT YOU LIVE WITH SOMEONE VERY SIMILAR TO THAT EVERYDAY.
When he gets an idea he thinks is fun...
THREE'S A BIG DIFFER-ENCE!!
I'LL STAY IN THIS GUY'S ROOM.
HUH? IS SHE A FRIEND OF HASU-KAWA'S?
Hey, his girlfriend, maybe?
I DON'T KNOW HER!
WHY DO I—
NO ONE IS TELLING YOU THAT SHE HAS TO SLEEP INSIDE YOUR ROOM.
OF COURSE NOT!!
210
I DON'T BELIEVE IT.
WHY TODAY OF ALL DAYS?
Fate sure is selfish!! ★

IF MITSURU WERE HERE, THEN...
THERE WASN'T *REALLY* ANY GOOD REASON FOR HIM TO PICK UP AND GO HOME, RIGHT?
BUT WHY WOULD A LITTLE GIRL GO INTO A BOYS' DORM?
!
WHAT'S YOUR NAME?!
WHO IN THIS DORM DO YOU KNOW?!
Return of Chronos
...
DING DONG DING DONG DING DONG
HASUKAWA!! TELEPHONE FOR YOU!
YOU STAY RIGHT HERE. GOT IT?
SHE COULD HAVE BEEN A GUY AT LEAST!

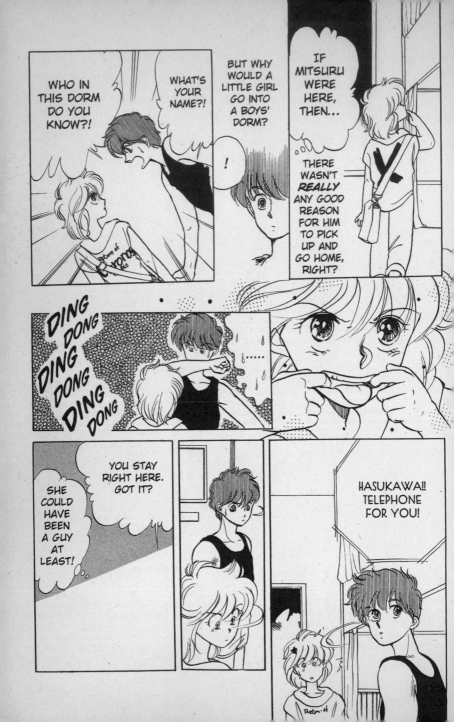

HELLO?
OH, SUKA-CHAN! IT'S ME! IT'S ME!
OH, THANK GOD! I TRIED TO CALL SO MANY TIMES, BUT NOBODY WOULD ANSWER!
... SHUN?
HEY!!
I'M WONDERING IF REINA IS THERE?
W-WAIT A MINUTE! IS THIS REINA...
I KNEW THE KID WOULD TRY THAT! WHERE? WHERE IS REINA NOW?!
WAIT A SECOND! ARE YOU SAYING THAT THIS GIRL IS ...
...YOUR LITTLE BROTHER?!
EXACTLY! I'M SURPRISED YOU FIGURED IT OUT!
...TO BE CONTINUED.

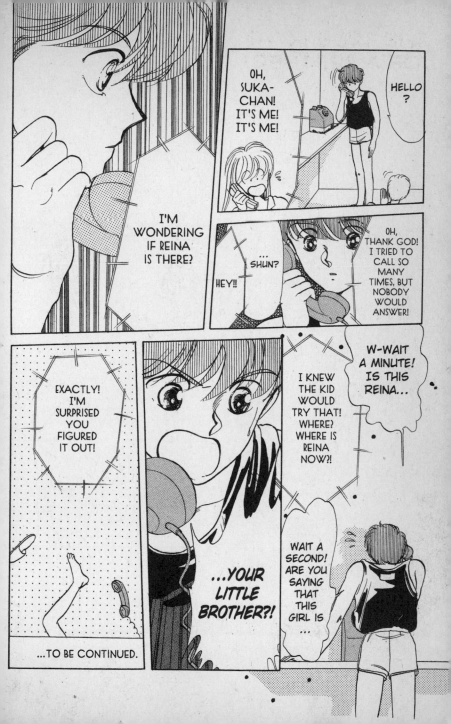

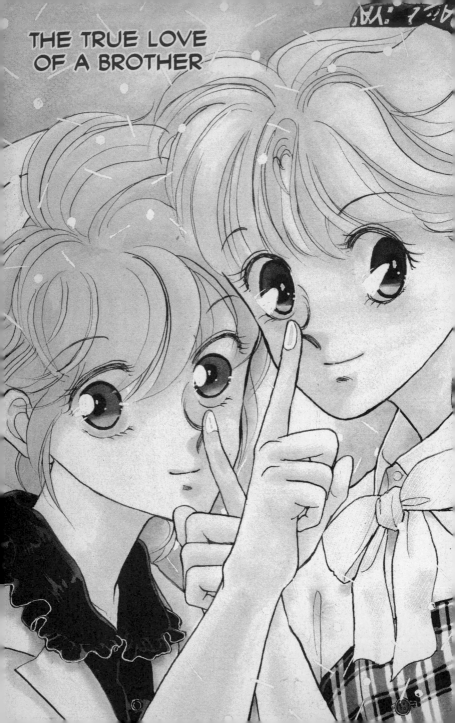

THE TRUE LOVE
OF A BROTHER

WHO THE HECK IS THIS?

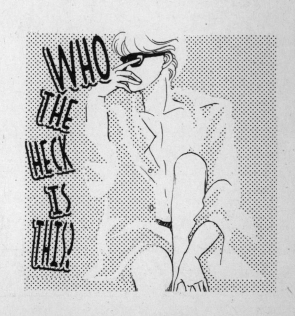

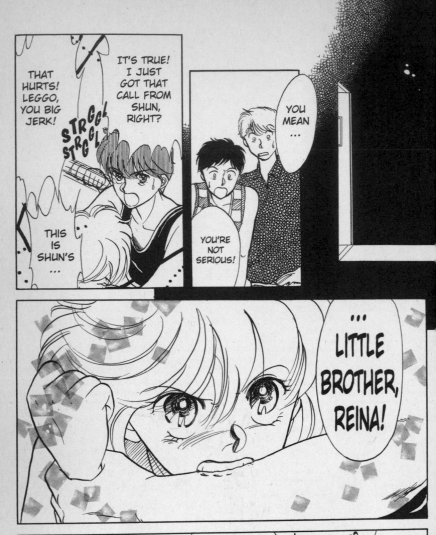

THAT HURTS! LEGGO, YOU BIG JERK!

IT'S TRUE! I JUST GOT THAT CALL FROM SHUN, RIGHT?

YOU MEAN ...

STRGGL STRGGL

THIS IS SHUN'S ...

YOU'RE NOT SERIOUS!

... LITTLE BROTHER, REINA!

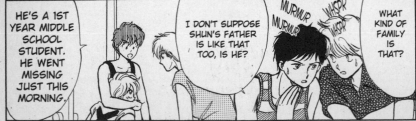

HE'S A 1ST YEAR MIDDLE SCHOOL STUDENT. HE WENT MISSING JUST THIS MORNING.

I DON'T SUPPOSE SHUN'S FATHER IS LIKE THAT TOO, IS HE?

MURMUR MURMUR

WHSPR WSPR

WHAT KIND OF FAMILY IS THAT?

I NEVER TOLD ANY LIES! I JUST KEPT QUIET!
SO THAT'S WHY HE WANTED TO GO TO HASUKAWA'S ROOM.
SHUN LIVES IN SHI-ZUOKA, RIGHT? HE CAME A LONG WAY ON HIS OWN.
IT'S SUMMER VACATION! I THOUGHT NOBODY WOULD BE IN THE DORM!
THAT MAKES SENSE.
IF THAT'S THE CASE, WE CAN ALLOW HIM TO STAY.
HASUKAWA, HE'S IN YOUR HANDS.
DON'T JOKE LIKE THAT!
SHUN'S BROTHER IS THE SON OF A COMPANY PRESIDENT!
WHY DO I HAVE TO BE THE ONE TO BABYSIT SOMEONE WHO IS SO MUCH TROUBLE?
PREJUDICED AGAINST THE RICH.
HEY!
C'MON, HEY!

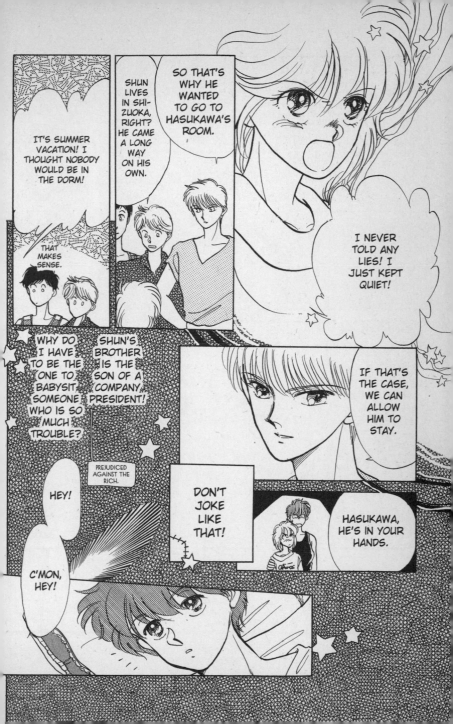

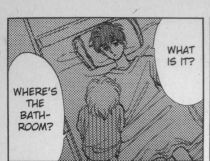

WHAT IS IT?
WHERE'S THE BATHROOM?
GO LEFT OUTSIDE THE DOOR. IT'S JUST DOWN THE HALL.
A COMPLETELY DIFFERENT ATTITUDE.
.....
HEY!
I CAN'T FIGURE THAT OUT! HEY!
I SAID, "HEY!"
SHAKE
SHAKE
GO TO THE BATHROOM ON YOUR *OWN*, WILL YOU?!
WAAAAHH!!
HEY, ARE YOU THERE?
STAY THERE, OKAY?
DON'T YOU GO BACK WITHOUT ME!
I'M HERE, SO SHUT UP AND FINISH!

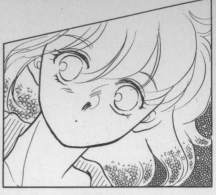

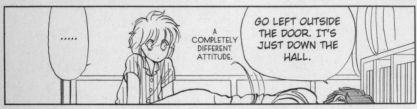

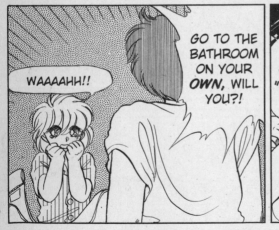

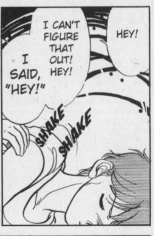

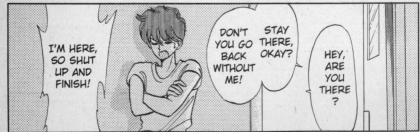

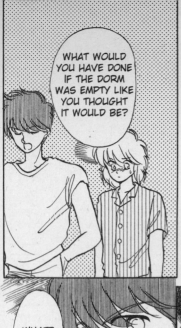

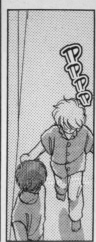

I DON'T CARE WHOSE KID HE IS—A 12-YEAR-OLD SHOULD BE ABLE TO GO TO THE BATHROOM ALONE!
AFTER MOM DIED, KAZU-HIRO DIDN'T DO THIS FOR ME—NOT EVEN ONCE!
TP TP TP TP
WHAT WOULD YOU HAVE DONE IF THE DORM WAS EMPTY LIKE YOU THOUGHT IT WOULD BE?
GRR
KIDS WHO CAN'T GO TO THE BATHROOM ALONE SHOULDN'T GO RUNNING AWAY IN THE FIRST PLACE! GOD, HOW STUPID!
WHAT?
BAM
BAM BAM
IF YOU WANT TO SLEEP IN THE HALL, GO RIGHT AHEAD.
WAAHH!
LET ME IN!!
Kazuya, you little idiot! Afraid of ghosts?
I'M GONNA TELL ON YOU!
SNIFF!
The only ghost that can appear here would be mom!
Oh! You're right.

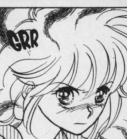

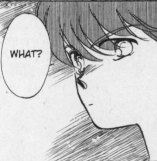

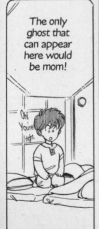

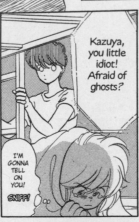

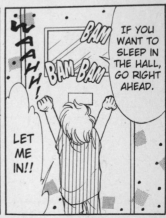

YOU SAY THAT SHUN'S LITTLE BROTHER IS HERE?
TMP TMP TMP
WHERE?
WHEN DID HE GET HERE?
WELL... I GUESS IT FIGURES.
THAT'S SHUN'S BROTHER, ALL RIGHT.
STILL HALF ASLEEP AND DOESN'T KNOW WHAT'S GOING ON.
ALL RIGHT. OUT OF THE WAY.
HE'S NOT ON DISPLAY.

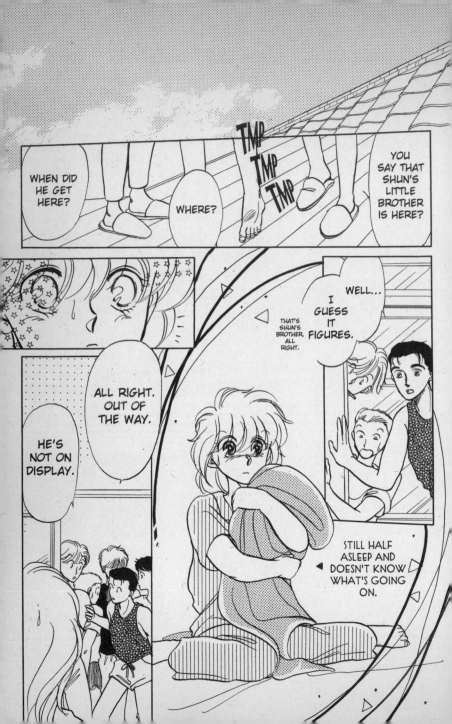

SO, YOU'RE FINALLY UP?
YOU SLEEP PRETTY LATE FOR A FREE-LOADER.
BREAK-FAST!
I DON'T WANT *THIS* FOR BREAK-FAST!
OKAY, STARVE.
FIP
GRRU GRRU GRRU
200ml
THE CAFETERIA ONLY HAS ENOUGH FOR THE PEOPLE HERE. WE DON'T HAVE EXTRA FOR YOU!
I'M A GUEST HERE! YOU SHOULD TREAT A LITTLE KID BET—
WHO IS?
A *GUEST*, YOU SAY?

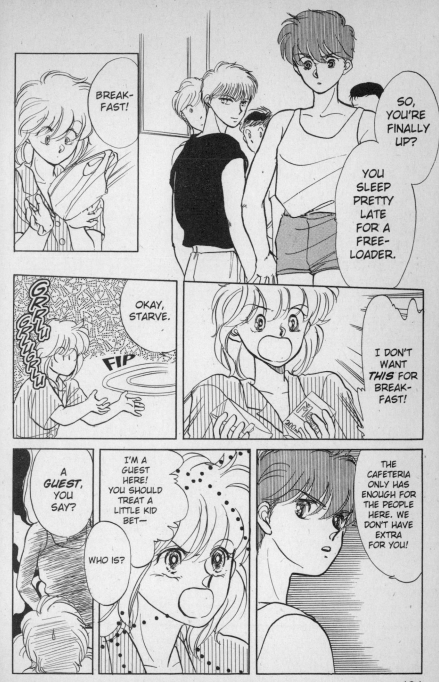

DON'T JUST SIT THERE!!
Men's Room
WHO RUNS AWAY WITHOUT A TOOTH-BRUSH?!
YOU IDIOT!
IF YOU GO THERE, THE DORM MOTHER WILL FIND YOU!
IT'S AGAINST THE RULES TO ALLOW NON-RESIDENTS TO SLEEP HERE!
ACTUALLY, HE'S PRETTY GOOD AT BABYSITTING.
ALTHOUGH IT LOOKS LIKE HE'S ONLY VENTING HIS ANGER ON THE KID.
IT'S HOT!
HEY, DON'T YOU HAVE AN AIR CONDI-TIONER?
WHO COULD AFFORD SOMETHING THAT EXPENSIVE?
Chronos

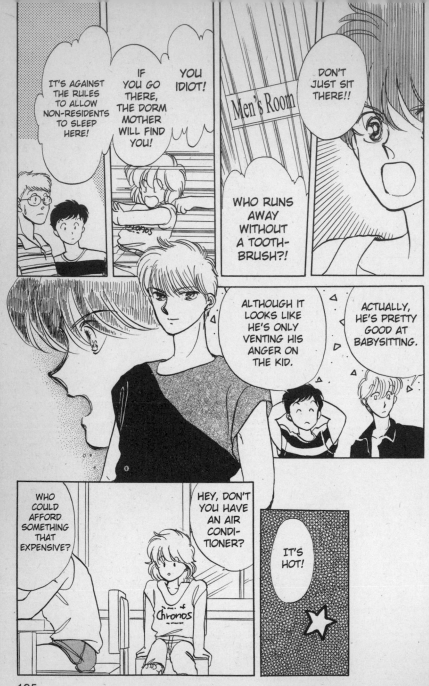

THE BATHS ARE ONLY OPEN DURING CERTAIN HOURS.
I WANNA TAKE A BATH.
.....
OUR HOUSE IS SO MUCH BETTER!
HOW CAN MY BROTHER STAND TO LIVE IN SUCH A PLACE?
THEN WHY DID YOU RUN AWAY?
GRRRRRR
YOUR ABSENCE CAN ONLY MAKE THINGS EASIER FOR THEM.
YOU'RE WRONG, YOU BIG MEANIE!
KACHIK

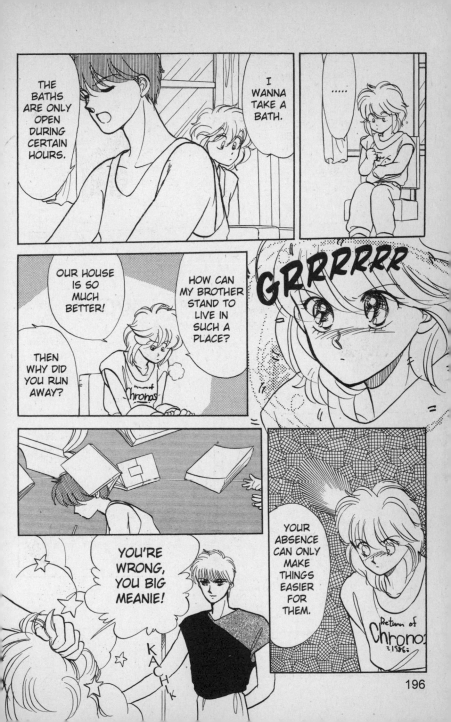

SHUN'S COMING TO GET YOU, SO BE GOOD AND GO BACK WITH HIM.
HE SAID HE'D PROBABLY BE HERE BEFORE NOON.
WHEN DID SHUN SAY HE'D COME?
NO!!
HE'S COME ALL THIS WAY FOR YOU! YOU CAN AT LEAST WAIT HERE TO MEET HIM.
NOBODY HAS ANYTHING TO DO, SO THEY ALL CAME OUT TO WATCH.
YOU DON'T REALIZE YOUR SITUATION, DO YOU?
OWWW!
I'M SHORRY!

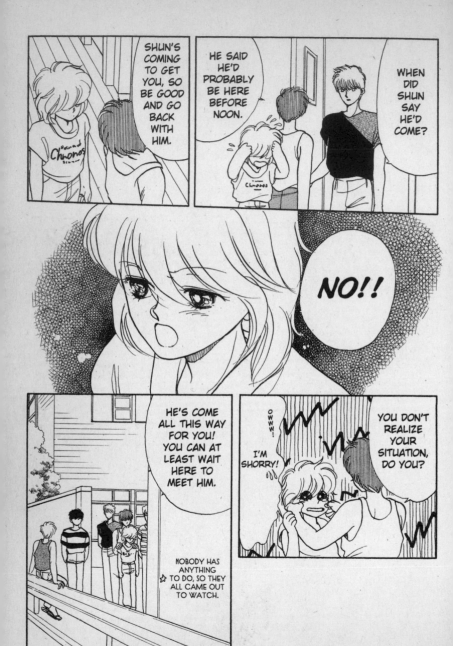

WHY NOT?
I DIDN'T WANT ANYBODY TO COME FOR ME!
MOMMY... DADDY... NOBODY WANTS ME!!
I'M JUST IN THE WAY WHEN I'M THERE!
SLAPP
OUCH ...
BONK
LISTEN, YOU--
WHAT ARE YOU DOING TO MY LITTLE REINA?!
REINA!!

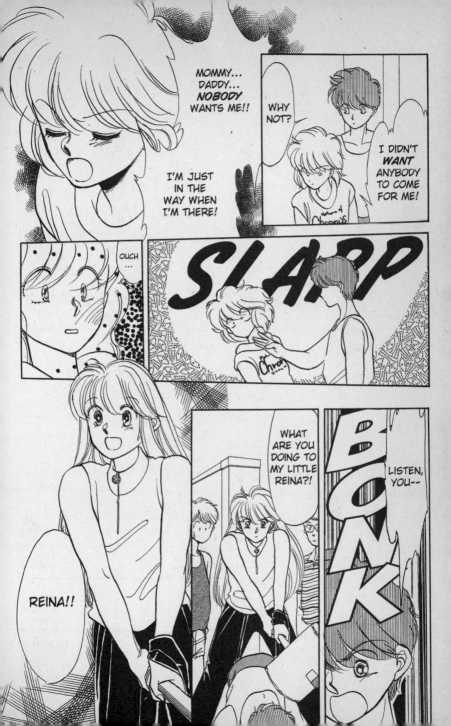

ONII-CHAMA!!
WHAT'S WRONG?
SHLUMP
IF YOU DON'T KNOW, YOU'LL NEVER KNOW.
YOU MADE EVERY-BODY WORRY!
YOU BAD BOY!
SNIFF
ONII-CHAMA!

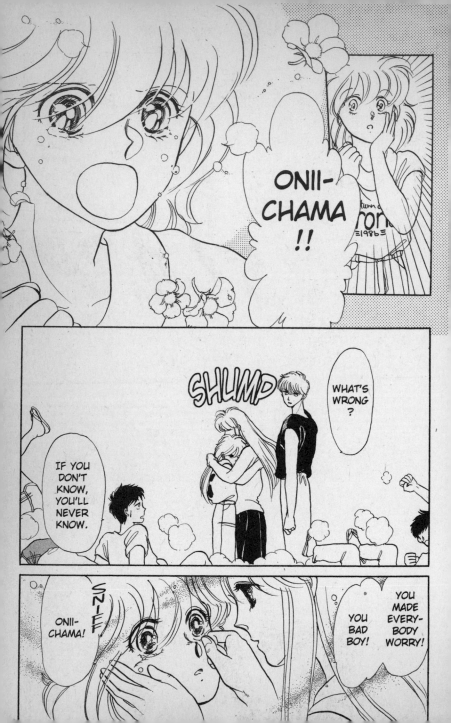

YOU FOUND THE DORM RIGHT AWAY? YOU DIDN'T GET LOST?
There, there...
SNIFF SNIFF
LISTEN! LISTEN! I WAS SO SCARED!
THE TRAIN STATION WAS SO BIG!
....
TH-THERE'S NOTHING WEIRD HERE, RIGHT?
THAT'S HOW BROTHERS ACT, RIGHT?
RIGHT! NO MATTER HOW IT LOOKS, THEY'RE BOTH GUYS!
BUT IT'S A *LITTLE* WEIRD, DON'T YOU THINK?
PRE-TENDING TO SLEEP.
PRE-TENDING NOT TO NOTICE.
SUKA-CHAN!
HUH?
GRMP
THANKS FOR LOOKING AFTER REINA!
AND THANK YOU, EVERYONE.
BOW

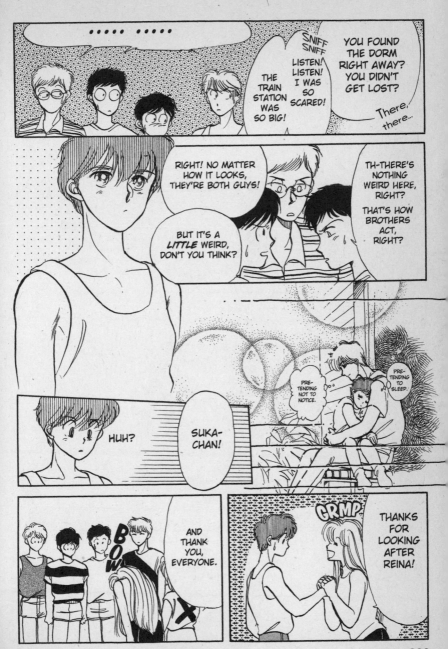

YUI WAS JUST BORN AND MOMMY TIRES SO EASILY, SO WE REALLY SHOULDN'T STRESS HER OUT EVEN MORE.
NOW, REINA, WE'RE GOING HOME.
YOU'RE A *DUMMY!!*
SO YOU— YOU'RE JUST LIKE THE REST OF THEM!!
REINA?
REINA...
SHUN. YOU KNOW WHY THE KID RAN AWAY, RIGHT?
GRAB

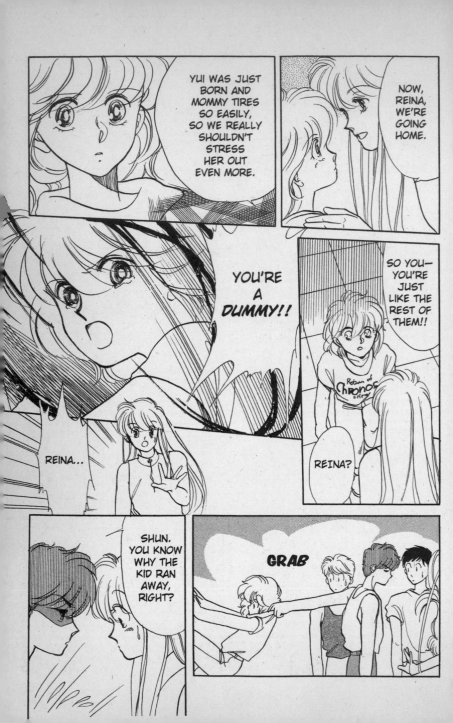

OH, REALLY? SHUN KISARAGI'S LITTLE BROTHER? HOW CUTE YOU ARE! YOU JUST GOT HERE? I THINK I CAN MAKE AN EXCEPTION THIS ONE TIME!
DORM MOTHER
UM... YEAH... I GUESS.
210
MOMMY JUST GAVE BIRTH TO OUR LITTLE SISTER.
SISTER?!
SHE'S CALLED YUI.
SHE'S REALLY CUTE! ♡
THAT'S A LOT OF YEARS BET-WEEN YOU!
BUT MOMMY'S ONLY 35-YEARS-OLD!
THAT'S WHY...
... ONII-CHAMA AND REINA AREN'T WANTED ANYMORE!
FIVE-YEAR-OLDS THINK LIKE THAT? AND *THAT'S* WHY YOU RAN AWAY?!
DON'T HIT OTHER PEOPLE'S KIDS!

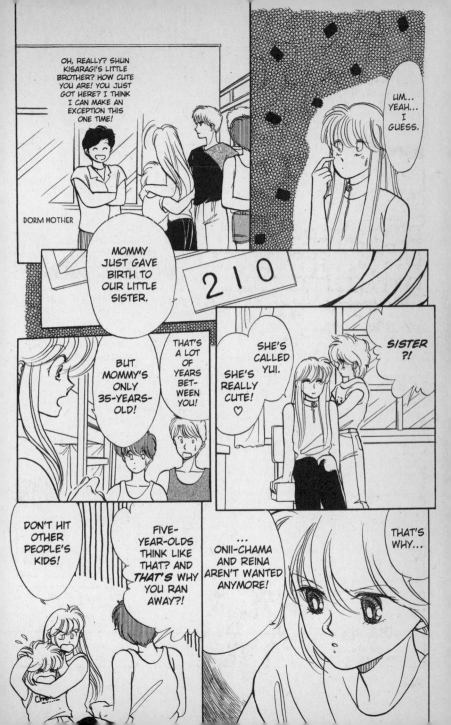

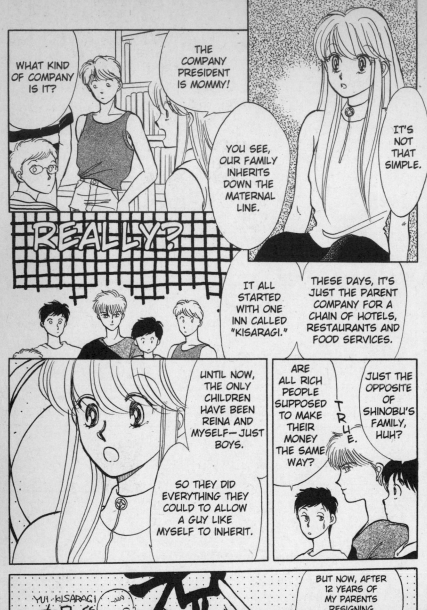

WHAT KIND OF COMPANY IS IT?
THE COMPANY PRESIDENT IS MOMMY!
IT'S NOT THAT SIMPLE.
YOU SEE, OUR FAMILY INHERITS DOWN THE MATERNAL LINE.
REALLY?
THESE DAYS, IT'S JUST THE PARENT COMPANY FOR A CHAIN OF HOTELS, RESTAURANTS AND FOOD SERVICES.
IT ALL STARTED WITH ONE INN CALLED "KISARAGI."
JUST THE OPPOSITE OF SHINOBU'S FAMILY, HUH?
TRUE.
ARE ALL RICH PEOPLE SUPPOSED TO MAKE THEIR MONEY THE SAME WAY?
UNTIL NOW, THE ONLY CHILDREN HAVE BEEN REINA AND MYSELF— JUST BOYS.
SO THEY DID EVERYTHING THEY COULD TO ALLOW A GUY LIKE MYSELF TO INHERIT.
BUT NOW, AFTER 12 YEARS OF MY PARENTS RESIGNING THEMSELVES TO FATE, A GIRL IS BORN.
YUI KISARAGI
如月唯
生後1週間
ONE WEEK OLD

(Congratulations)

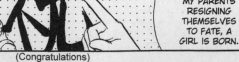

MOMMY AND DADDY ARE JUST AWFUL!
EVER SINCE YUI WAS BORN, IT'S BEEN "YUI, YUI," ALL THE TIME!
Coochy-coo!
What a good baby!
THEY COMPLETELY FORGOT HOW HARD YOU WORKED TO DO THE THINGS THEY WANTED, ONII-CHAMA!
BUT YOU DON'T GET ANGRY AT ALL, DO YOU? AND YUI... YUI...
I THINK YUI IS JUST NO FAIR!!
IN OTHER WORDS, THIS RUNAWAY INCIDENT IS A MESSAGE TO YOUR FAMILY CONCERNING SHUN'S RIGHTS OF INHERITANCE?
AH! YOU CAN'T MEAN THAT...
...YOU'VE BEEN RAISED AS A GIRL SINCE CHILDHOOD SO YOU CAN INHERIT YOUR FAMILY'S FORTUNE?
I GET IT! NOW I CAN UNDERSTAND WHY SHUN'S HAIR IS SO LONG!
N-NO!
I JUST LIKED MY HAIR TOO MUCH TO CUT IT!
IT SUITS ME, AND LOOK HOW PRETTY IT IS!
BUT REINA, IT'S EXACTLY AS I SAID BEFORE.

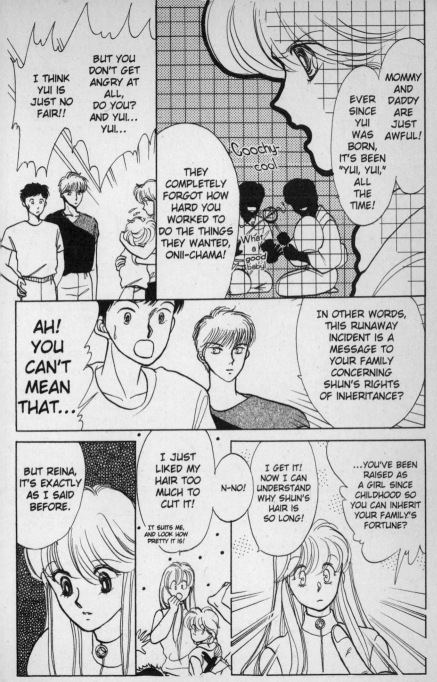

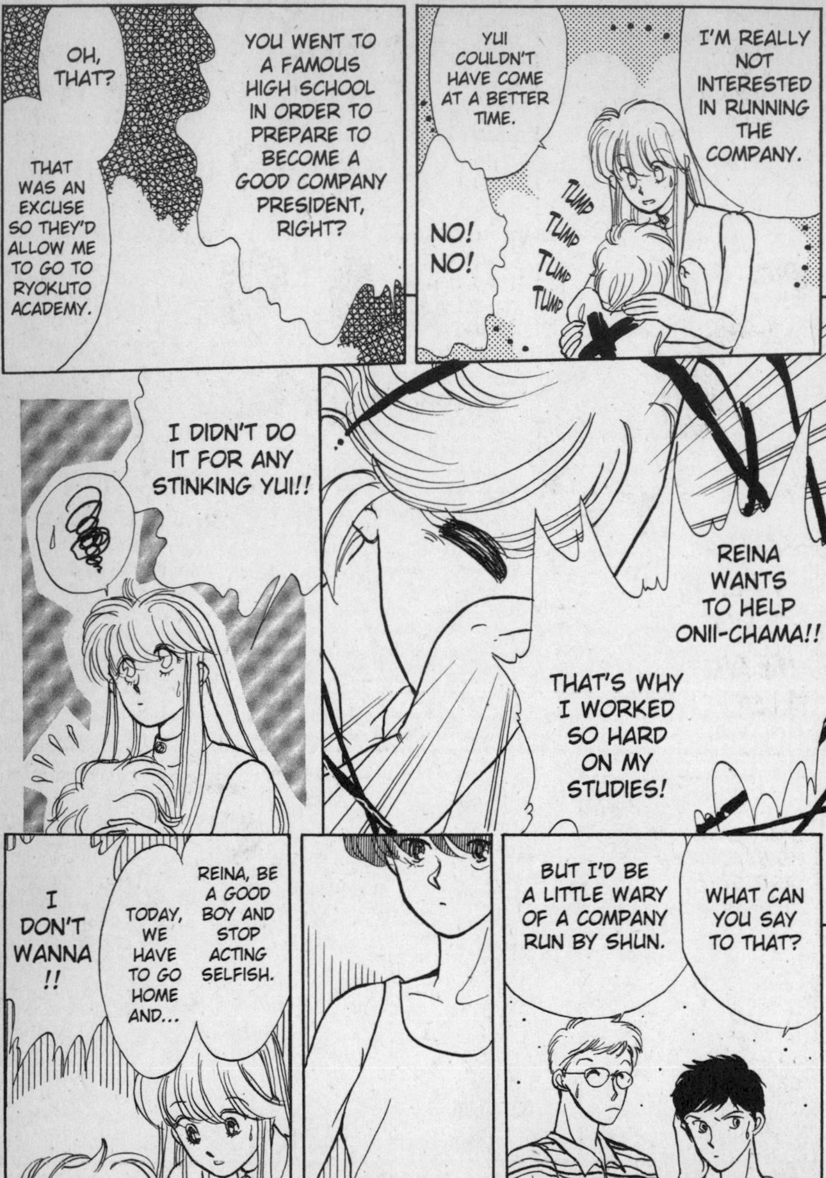
I'M REALLY NOT INTERESTED IN RUNNING THE COMPANY.
YUI COULDN'T HAVE COME AT A BETTER TIME.
NO! NO!
TUMP TUMP TUMP TUMP
YOU WENT TO A FAMOUS HIGH SCHOOL IN ORDER TO PREPARE TO BECOME A GOOD COMPANY PRESIDENT, RIGHT?
OH, THAT?
THAT WAS AN EXCUSE SO THEY'D ALLOW ME TO GO TO RYOKUTO ACADEMY.
REINA WANTS TO HELP ONII-CHAMA!!
THAT'S WHY I WORKED SO HARD ON MY STUDIES!
I DIDN'T DO IT FOR ANY STINKING YUI!!
WHAT CAN YOU SAY TO THAT?
BUT I'D BE A LITTLE WARY OF A COMPANY RUN BY SHUN.
REINA, BE A GOOD BOY AND STOP ACTING SELFISH.
TODAY, WE HAVE TO GO HOME AND...
I DON'T WANNA!!

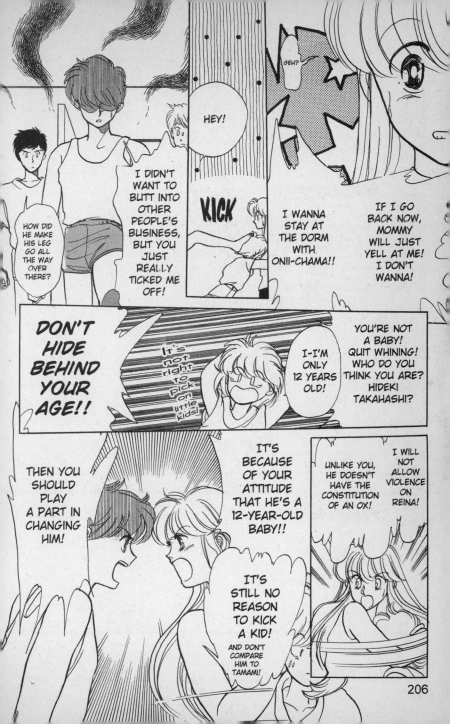

GEH?
IF I GO BACK NOW, MOMMY WILL JUST YELL AT ME! I DON'T WANNA!
I WANNA STAY AT THE DORM WITH ONII-CHAMA!!
HEY!
KICK
I DIDN'T WANT TO BUTT INTO OTHER PEOPLE'S BUSINESS, BUT YOU JUST REALLY TICKED ME OFF!
HOW DID HE MAKE HIS LEG GO ALL THE WAY OVER THERE?
YOU'RE NOT A BABY! QUIT WHINING! WHO DO YOU THINK YOU ARE? HIDEKI TAKAHASHI?
I-I'M ONLY 12 YEARS OLD!
It's not right to pick on little kids!
DON'T HIDE BEHIND YOUR AGE!!
I WILL NOT ALLOW VIOLENCE ON REINA!
UNLIKE YOU, HE DOESN'T HAVE THE CONSTITUTION OF AN OX!
IT'S BECAUSE OF YOUR ATTITUDE THAT HE'S A 12-YEAR-OLD BABY!!
THEN YOU SHOULD PLAY A PART IN CHANGING HIM!
IT'S STILL NO REASON TO KICK A KID!
AND DON'T COMPARE HIM TO TAMAMI!

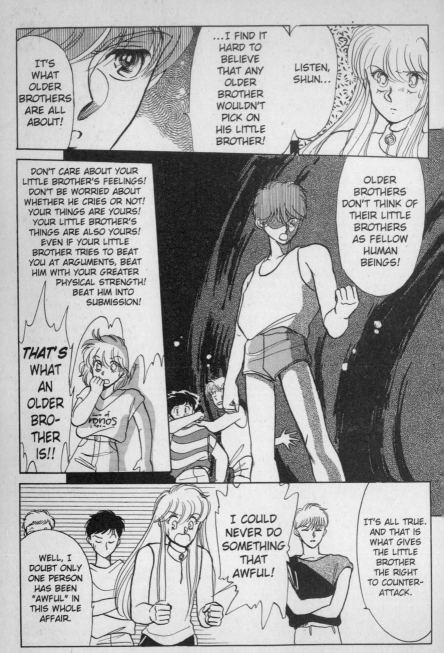

LISTEN, SHUN...
...I FIND IT HARD TO BELIEVE THAT ANY OLDER BROTHER WOULDN'T PICK ON HIS LITTLE BROTHER!
IT'S WHAT OLDER BROTHERS ARE ALL ABOUT!
OLDER BROTHERS DON'T THINK OF THEIR LITTLE BROTHERS AS FELLOW HUMAN BEINGS!
DON'T CARE ABOUT YOUR LITTLE BROTHER'S FEELINGS! DON'T BE WORRIED ABOUT WHETHER HE CRIES OR NOT! YOUR THINGS ARE YOURS! YOUR LITTLE BROTHER'S THINGS ARE ALSO YOURS! EVEN IF YOUR LITTLE BROTHER TRIES TO BEAT YOU AT ARGUMENTS, BEAT HIM WITH YOUR GREATER PHYSICAL STRENGTH! BEAT HIM INTO SUBMISSION!
THAT'S WHAT AN OLDER BRO-THER IS!!
IT'S ALL TRUE. AND THAT IS WHAT GIVES THE LITTLE BROTHER THE RIGHT TO COUNTER-ATTACK.
I COULD NEVER DO SOMETHING THAT AWFUL!
WELL, I DOUBT ONLY ONE PERSON HAS BEEN "AWFUL" IN THIS WHOLE AFFAIR.

OH, THAT'S RIGHT.
KAZUYA'S FAMILY WAS JUST TWO BROTHERS.
HEY! HOW DARE YOU TALK TO ONII-CHAMA ALL HIGH AND MIGHTY!!
BECAUSE I CAN'T STAND TO SEE HIM LIKE THIS.
HEEEEY!!
YOU *STILL* DON'T UNDERSTAND YOUR POSITION, DO YOU, KID?
GASP
HELP ME, ONII-CHAMA! HELP ME!
BUT ...
BUT I CAN'T...
I THINK AN OLDER BROTHER'S PURPOSE IS TO PROTECT HIS YOUNGER BROTHER AND SISTER!
IF THEY'RE ALWAYS PROTECTED, THEN THEY'LL TURN OUT WEAK!!
A STRANGER SHOULDN'T DO WHAT I DID, BUT IF *YOU* DON'T DO IT...
...WHO *IS* GOING TO BE THE ONE TO MAKE HIM CRY?!

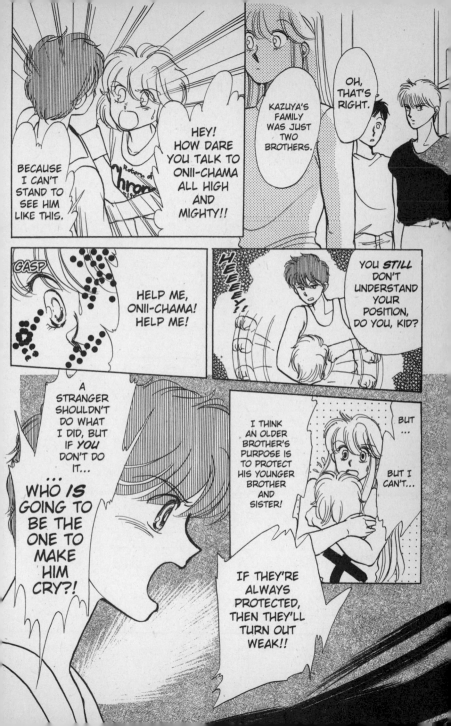

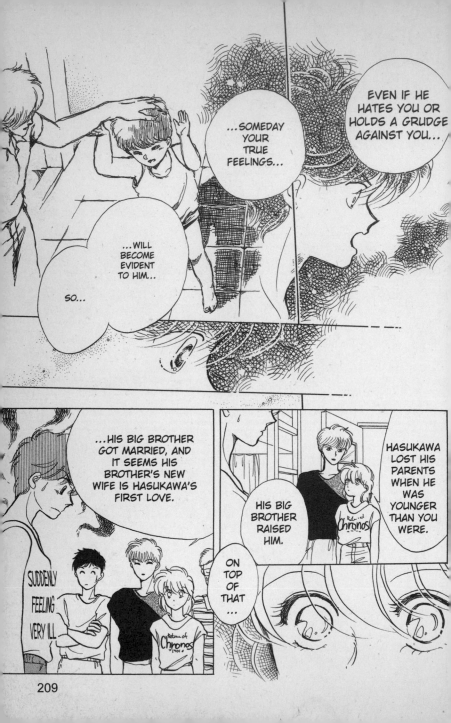

EVEN IF HE HATES YOU OR HOLDS A GRUDGE AGAINST YOU...
...SOMEDAY YOUR TRUE FEELINGS...
...WILL BECOME EVIDENT TO HIM...
SO...
HASUKAWA LOST HIS PARENTS WHEN HE WAS YOUNGER THAN YOU WERE.
HIS BIG BROTHER RAISED HIM.
ON TOP OF THAT ...
...HIS BIG BROTHER GOT MARRIED, AND IT SEEMS HIS BROTHER'S NEW WIFE IS HASUKAWA'S FIRST LOVE.
SUDDENLY FEELING VERY ILL

YOU POOR GUY!
I DON'T NEED *YOUR* SYMPATHY!
OKAY, SUKA-CHAN.
FROM NOW ON, I WON'T SPARE THE ROD OF TOUGH LOVE IN THE REARING OF REINA!
ARE YOU *SURE* YOU WANT TO TAKE ON SUCH A VIOLENT PHILOSOPHY?
SURE, IF IT MEANS THAT REINA CAN GROW UP TO BE SOMEONE AS STRONG AS SUKA-CHAN.
NOW, REINA, WE'RE GOING HOME!
GRUNT
O-OKAY. BUT...
MOMMY WILL BE REALLY MAD...
I'm scared
YOU'LL BE FINE.
WE'LL *BOTH* APOLOGIZE TO HER.
HAVEN'T YOU LEARNED *ANYTHING?!*

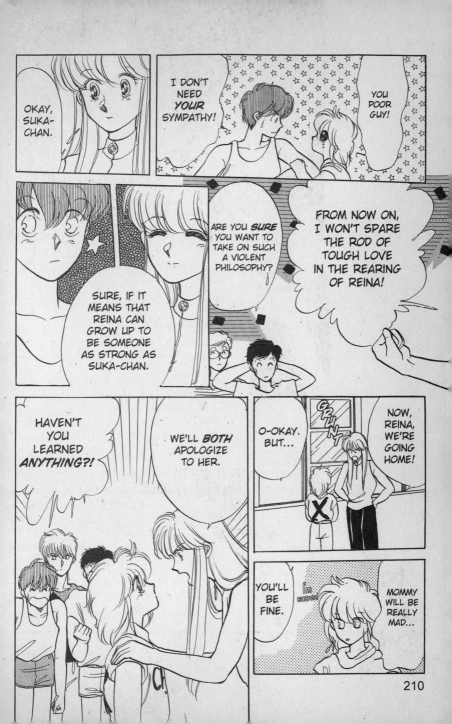

AND SO, THE KISARAGI BROTHERS WENT HOME.
See you!
MAYBE ONCE...
MAYBE JUST ONCE DURING SUMMER VACATION...
...I'LL GO HOME TO SEE HOW SUMIRE IS DOING.
I SEE. WHILE I WAS GONE...
...A LOT OF AMUSING THINGS WENT ON HERE.
TOO BAD I MISSED IT.
WHAT WAS AMUSING ABOUT IT?

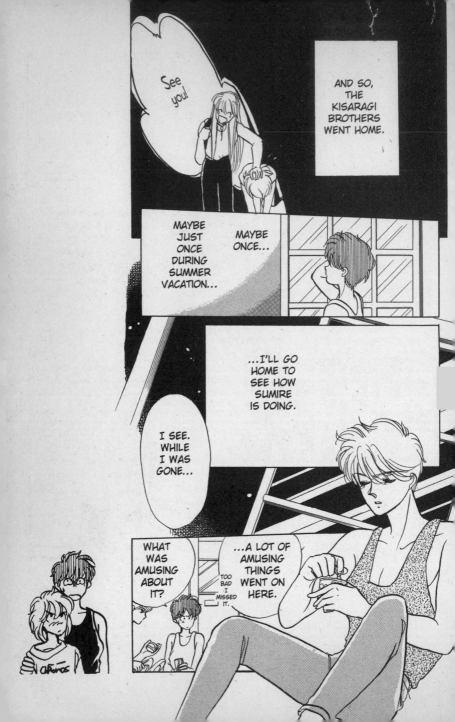

SEE?
I HAD TWO FUNERALS AND A 13TH-YEAR COMMEMORATION TO ATTEND.
YOU SHOULD HAVE BEEN HERE AT SUCH A CRUCIAL TIME!
I COULDN'T HELP IT!
IS THE IKEDA FAMILY ON THE ROAD TO EXTINCTION?
YOU IDIOT! IT WASN'T MY FAMILY, BUT FAMILIES WHO ATTEND OUR SERVICES!
DIDN'T I EVER TELL YOU?
MY FAMILY RUNS A TEMPLE.
EH?
EHHH?!
M-MIT-SURU...
...YOU'RE THE ELDEST SON OF A TEMPLE FAMILY?
YOU COULD SAY THAT.
THEN YOU INHERIT THE TEMPLE?

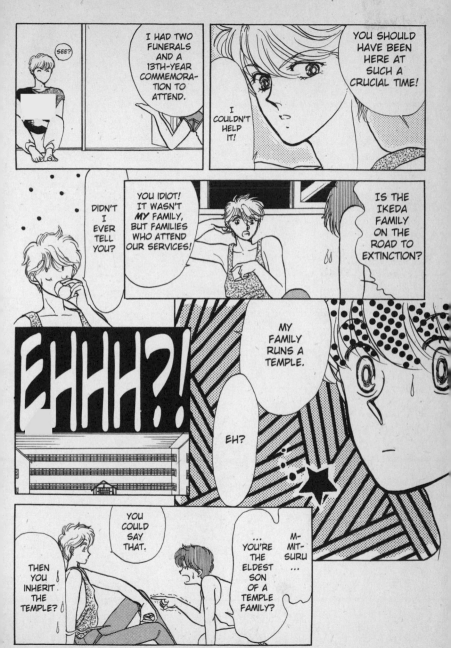

THE TRUE LOVE OF A BROTHER: THE END

COMPLETE OUR SURVEY AND LET US KNOW WHAT YOU THINK!

☐ Please do NOT send me information about VIZ products, news and events, special offers, or other information.

☐ Please do NOT send me information from VIZ's trusted business partners.

Name: _____

Address: _____

City: _____ State: _____ Zip: _____

E-mail: _____

☐ Male ☐ Female   Date of Birth (mm/dd/yyyy): ___ / ___ / ___   (Under 13? Parental consent required)

What race/ethnicity do you consider yourself? (please check one)

☐ Asian/Pacific Islander   ☐ Black/African American   ☐ Hispanic/Latino

☐ Native American/Alaskan Native ☐ White/Caucasian   ☐ Other: _____

What VIZ product did you purchase? (check all that apply and indicate title purchased)

☐ DVD/VHS _____

☐ Graphic Novel _____

☐ Magazines _____

☐ Merchandise _____

Reason for purchase: (check all that apply)

☐ Special offer   ☐ Favorite title   ☐ Gift

☐ Recommendation   ☐ Other _____

Where did you make your purchase? (please check one)

☐ Comic store   ☐ Bookstore   ☐ Mass/Grocery Store

☐ Newsstand   ☐ Video/Video Game Store ☐ Other: _____

☐ Online (site: _____)

What other VIZ properties have you purchased/own? _____

_____

How many anime and/or manga titles have you purchased in the last year? How many were VIZ titles? **(please check one from each column)**

ANIME	MANGA	VIZ
☐ None	☐ None	☐ None
☐ 1-4	☐ 1-4	☐ 1-4
☐ 5-10	☐ 5-10	☐ 5-10
☐ 11+	☐ 11+	☐ 11+

I find the pricing of VIZ products to be: **(please check one)**

☐ Cheap ☐ Reasonable ☐ Expensive

What genre of manga and anime would you like to see from VIZ? **(please check two)**

☐ Adventure ☐ Comic Strip ☐ Science Fiction ☐ Fighting

☐ Horror ☐ Romance ☐ Fantasy ☐ Sports

What do you think of VIZ's new look?

☐ Love It ☐ It's OK ☐ Hate It ☐ Didn't Notice ☐ No Opinion

Which do you prefer? **(please check one)**

☐ Reading right-to-left

☐ Reading left-to-right

Which do you prefer? **(please check one)**

☐ Sound effects in English

☐ Sound effects in Japanese with English captions

☐ Sound effects in Japanese only with a glossary at the back

THANK YOU! Please send the completed form to:

VIZ Survey
42 Catharine St.
Poughkeepsie, NY 12601

All information provided will be used for internal purposes only. We promise not to sell or otherwise divulge your information.

Translation Notes

Translation Note: Page 124—The reason one of the students was afraid there would be an extra one is because of an old Japanese ghost story where 10 friends tells ghost stories, and whenever they would do a headcount, there would always be 11.

Translation Note: Page 149—Sakutaro Hagiwara wrote a famous Japanese poem entitled "Oyogu Hito" (*The Swimming Man*).

Translation Note: Page 166—Horror Show is a reference to the movie *A Clockwork Orange*, where the words "Horror Show" (taken from a Russian homophone) means "good."

Translation Note: Page 199—"Onii-chama" is a childish way of saying "Onii-sama" (big brother) with a very respectful honorific attached. The honorific indicates respect, but the childishness indicates intimacy, so the nickname is contradictory.

Translation Note: Page 206—Hideki Takahashi is the actor who portrayed the main character in the movie Otoko no Monshô (*Emblem of a Man*) who was stuck between the destruction of his personal morals and his duty to serve his Yakuza Oyabun (boss) father. There is a resemblance between Takahashi's character and Al Pacino's character in *The Godfather*.

Translation Note: Page 206—Tamami was the main villain of a manga by horror master Kazuo Umezu called Akanbo Shôjo. Tamami is an adult stuck in a child's body (similar to the children in the movie *Akira*) and her bitterness and intelligence within the cute childlike features is the source of terror.

—William Flanagan

shojo

AT THE HEART OF THE MATTER

- Alice 19th
- Angel Sanctuary
- Banana Fish
- Basara
- B.B. Explosion
- Boys Over Flowers *
- Ceres, Celestial Legend *
- Descendants of Darkness
- Dolls
- From Far Away
- Fushigi Yûgi
- Hana-Kimi
- Here Is Greenwood
- Hot Gimmick
- Imadoki
- Kare First Love
- Please Save My Earth *
- Red River
- Revolutionary Girl Utena
- Sensual Phrase
- W Juliet
- Wedding Peach
- Wild Com.
- X/1999

Start Your Shôjo Graphic Novel Collection Today!

FRESH FROM JAPAN™ 日本最新 VIZ

www.viz.com

STARTING @ $9.95!

*Also available on DVD from VIZ

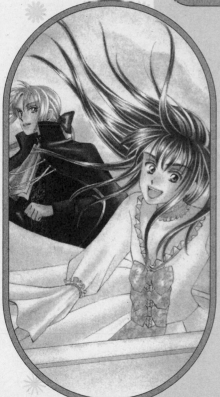

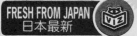